P9-DME-061

HOW TO SAY IT®
to Get into the College of Your Choice

PCTA
Library Media Center
41 Fricker Street
Providence, RI 02903

Also by Linda Metcalf, Ph.D.

THE MIRACLE QUESTION
SOLUTION FOCUSED GROUP THERAPY
TEACHING TOWARD SOLUTIONS
PARENTING TOWARD SOLUTIONS
COUNSELING TOWARD SOLUTIONS

41 Fricker Street

HOW TO SAY IT®
to Get into the College of Your Choice

Application, Essay, and Interview
Strategies to Get You the Big Envelope

Linda Metcalf, Ph.D.

PRENTICE HALL PRESS

PRENTICE HALL PRESS
Published by the Penguin Group
Penguin Group (USA) Inc.
375 Hudson Street, New York, New York 10014, USA
Penguin Group (Canada), 90 Eglinton Avenue East, Suite 700, Toronto, Ontario M4P 2Y3, Canada
(a division of Pearson Penguin Canada Inc.)
Penguin Books Ltd., 80 Strand, London WC2R 0RL, England
Penguin Group Ireland, 25 St. Stephen's Green, Dublin 2, Ireland (a division of Penguin Books Ltd.)
Penguin Group (Australia), 250 Camberwell Road, Camberwell, Victoria 3124, Australia
(a division of Pearson Australia Group Pty. Ltd.)
Penguin Books India Pvt. Ltd., 11 Community Centre, Panchsheel Park, New Delhi—110 017, India
Penguin Group (NZ), 67 Apollo Drive, Rosedale, North Shore 0745, Auckland, New Zealand
(a division of Pearson New Zealand Ltd.)
Penguin Books (South Africa) (Pty.) Ltd., 24 Sturdee Avenue, Rosebank, Johannesburg 2196, South Africa

Penguin Books Ltd., Registered Offices: 80 Strand, London WC2R 0RL, England

While the author has made every effort to provide accurate telephone members and Internet addresses at the time of publication, neither the publisher nor the author assumes any responsibility for errors, or for changes that occur after publication. Further, the publisher does not have any control over and does not assume any responsibility for author or third-party websites or their content.

Copyright © 2007 by Linda Metcalf
Cover art by Paul Howalt
Cover design by Ben Gibson
Text design by Tiffany Estreicher

All rights reserved.
No part of this book may be reproduced, scanned, or distributed in any printed or electronic form without permission. Please do not participate in or encourage piracy of copyrighted materials in violation of the author's rights. Purchase only authorized editions.
PRENTICE HALL is a registered trademark of Penguin Group (USA) Inc.

First edition: June 2007

Library of Congress Cataloging-in-Publication Data

Metcalf, Linda.
   How to say it to get into the college of your choice : application, essay, and interview strategies to get you the big envelope / Linda Metcalf.
      p. cm.
    ISBN 978-0-7352-0420-1
  1. College applications—United States. 2. Universities and colleges—United States—Admission. 3. Exposition (Rhetoric) I. Title.
    LB2351.2.M47 2007
    378.1'664—dc22

                                                                                    2007003058

PRINTED IN THE UNITED STATES OF AMERICA

10   9   8   7   6   5   4   3   2

Most Prentice Hall books are available at special quantity discounts for bulk purchases, for sales promotions, premiums, fund-raising, or educational use. Special books, or book excerpts, can also be created to fit specific needs. For details, write: Special Markets, Penguin Group (USA) Inc., 375 Hudson Street, New York, New York 10014.

To my children, Roger Jr., Kelli, and Ryan,
all college graduates,
carpe diem!

To my husband, Roger,
your belief that everyone needs to keep learning
keeps us all striving for success.

CONTENTS

ACKNOWLEDGMENTS

Many of you will soon begin to reminisce about the people in your life that "made the difference that made the difference" and encouraged you to apply to college. As an author, I find myself also gathering those people in my heart that helped me through the process of writing this book. Sitting down to pound out the words is easy. But making the words make sense so that you, the reader, get what you need to make the next few years your best is a challenge that I do not take lightly. I have always been accused of being a student advocate and for that, I am quite proud. This book is for you.

Books are collections of the efforts of many people. Thank you, first, to Jeanette Shaw, whose guidance and editing at Prentice Hall assisted me in writing a book that is quite different from my previous ones. I appreciate your patience and excellent comments that helped to strengthen the book's purpose and give it a voice that encourages students everywhere that they *can* get into college once they know "how to say it."

Many thanks to Ryan Rose Weaver for her amazing ability to craft sentences about essays in a manner that makes any reader confident to take on the task. Your professional approach to this project during your senior year of college, when you had other projects and limited time, convinced me that your future is bright. Emerson College is soon to have an alumnus that will make them proud, and the literary world, a new writer to appreciate and watch!

Thanks also to Billee Molarte, a doctoral student at Texas Woman's University for her research and interviewing techniques with colleges across the nation. You helped me to gather data that will serve high school seniors with the answers they need the most.

Thank you to Ellen Coleman, my agent, who encouraged me to take on this project and helped me to grow as an author. As an educator at heart, this book is a special delivery for the people most dear to me professionally . . . the students.

Last, thank you to my children, who, although now living miles from home doing what they love, always get involved (because I always involve you!) through conversations and opinions that keep me sane. And to my husband: How can I forget the trips to the bookstores to get "one more college resource book"? Your loyalty to Baylor is a sure sign of what this book is written about and I hope every student that goes to the college of their dreams recalls their experience as fondly as you do. And to Rex I and Rex II, our golden retrievers who fill our time since our children have moved out and into the world, it's finally time to take that walk.

INTRODUCTION

Somewhere in a community such as yours, conversations are happening between parents, school counselors, and high school students about college. Many of those conversations will be well informed and many will not. Some of the conversations will involve emotions, dreams, and future professions and others will involve concerns about finances and location. A few conversations will focus on grades and others will focus on legacy, internships, and fraternities. Everyone involved in the conversations will have questions, opinions, and advice. Everyone will be looking at the future . . . your future. There will be lots of opinions on where to apply, when to apply, and how/when to respond and accept if admission is offered. In other words, the focus will be on the process of college applications and getting into the college of your choice.

But what might be left out of these somewhat challenging and informative conversations are what the conversations themselves are composed of . . . which words should be used, which phrases should be included, and what style of writing conveys the student's personality and the qualifications that make her the dream applicant. Choosing a college means more than choosing a career path; it means choosing a new home for the next four years that will be compatible with a student's personality and academic potential.

How to Say It to Get into the College of Your Choice is written for high school students, parents, teachers, school counselors, and other professionals who work with youth. Within this book, readers will get a firsthand glance inside the minds of admissions directors who were interviewed for this book and gave specific suggestions regarding what they look for in an applicant. Those suggestions are integrated into each chapter of this book, providing direct access to a successful college application process. This book is a guide for choosing the appropriate college, preparing for the SAT or ACT, and composing a dynamite essay for the exam. It will help students to accurately and effectively complete college applications and compose a descriptive and attractive résumé for letters of recommendation. The reader will also learn how to write the most impressive, powerful, and grammatically correct college essay and successfully interview in an impressive manner with college admission staff.

To accomplish these important tasks more easily, this book will provide words and phrases to use that define who the student is and what the student has accomplished during the high school years. Idea-generating questions and checklists are included to help the student identify certain aspects of a college that will match their personality, needs, and educational aspirations. These resources will be positioned in the form of lists and sample sentences at key points throughout the book that make for easy and immediate access. The reader will learn how to explore and express who he is, who he plans on becoming, and how he will add to the college culture. And finally, at the end of each chapter, a section titled College Clues and Cues is included as an afterthought of advice for the new high school graduate. These bits of information give you some hands-on advice on mastering the content of each chapter.

For the parents of a future scholar, there are tips given at the end of each chapter called College Clues and Cues for Parents that explain how to become a helpful coach during this all-important launching of the adolescent and how to encourage the adolescent in regard to planning strategies and deadlines. This book will cover some simple strategies to use that help parents identify how their adolescent "ticks" and what it will take to get them on their way out the door and into college.

A Final Word to the Aspiring College Student

This is the beginning of the best year of your life: freshman year, when there are no curfews (most of the time), no parents to make you study (unless they call you every day . . . but then, no one will be there to tell you to answer the phone), and new friends who share in your vision of a college diploma (and the right fraternity). Get ready for midnight study groups and professors that push you to think beyond what you thought you were capable of. Field trips, language labs, business competitions, art galleries, term papers, and literature assignments will pique your interest and challenge you to study much harder than you did in high school. A new roommate from across the country may become your best friend for life. Struggling will never be more fun. Learning will never be more challenging. And chances are, with the right decisions, you will love every second.

A Final Word to the Aspiring College Student

And the Finalists Are:
The Brightest, the Committed,
and the Honest

Carpe diem. Seize the day, boys.
Make your lives extraordinary.
—*Dead Poets Society*

So, here's the good news: At any given moment in the country, 95 percent of the colleges and universities are clamoring for your application. That is, all 17 million of you, who are looking to attend about 4,200 *colleges* in the United States during the next few years (Gill, p. 72). They hold marketing meetings, print up brochures and posters to get your attention, and race to college nights on your high school campus with free pens to pass out along with their applications. They offer *scholarships* and programs to meet your needs so that you will honor them by saying "yes." They conference over the endless applications that they receive and tailor their freshman class out of the brightest, the most committed, and the most honest students that apply. They want a diverse group to inspire the campus life and to bring credibility to their community. They want you as much as you want them.

But with so many choices, how do you hook up with the right school? Let's start by looking at what today's colleges and *universities* are looking for.

The following stories are examples of how students approached the college admission game. While they were successful at getting in, only two were successful at finishing the school where they started. The issues that emerge in the stories are lessons to pay attention to as you begin the most important game of your life.

The Brightest: Steven

"You have a real gift for writing," said Steven's senior *AP* English teacher, one day after everyone had left class. "I hope that you will look into college and consider teaching someday since you do so well in our class discussions." Steven smiled and sighed as he left the classroom. The inspiration was there as well as the motivation but Steven saw no way that he could attend college. Both of his parents were blue-collar workers who did little to encourage Steven to go to college. In fact, they saw him as someone who could help them "make ends meet" when he finished high school and got a job.

With little knowledge about financial aid and scholarships available for someone with his high GPA of 3.9, he still took the *SAT* test with a fee waiver at my encouragement. When his excellent SAT scores came in the mail, I told Steven that he had many options and helped him fill out the *Common Application*. I encouraged him to list his many extracurricular activities, which included Key Club, the National Honor Society, student council, and being a football trainer for three years. From the résumé he compiled using a form that I had given to him, I learned that he had an impressive job record, beginning at age fifteen when he began working at Six Flags Over Texas. During the years he worked at Six Flags, he had been promoted to manager of a retail shop by his senior year. This impressive job record would convey his determination and dependability.

Steven chose his two AP teachers, a youth-group leader, his supervisor at Six Flags, and the football coach as people that he felt would provide him with positive letters of recommendation. He also asked the same people to be references for various scholarships that he qualified for. He told each of his references about his dreams to be an English teacher in his request letter and said that he valued their opinion and needed their support. They complied with his request. His letters of recommendation described Steven as "bright, intelligent, articulate, responsible, driven, a team player, motivated, and future-oriented." The race was on and Steven was sure to win! He sent each person a thank-you note and sent in his applications to three state universities and one private university. His college essay included comments on how he had been inspired by those who recommended him, and how his parents had not had opportunities to attend college and his hope to set the stage for his younger sister to go to college. His words were eloquent, descriptive, and clearly described his personal story in a way that won my heart and apparently those of the admissions directors.

In March of his senior year, Steven was awarded a full academic scholarship to a top private university in Texas with a proposed major in English. His parents were shocked that their son had received such an offer. They proudly told everyone they knew about their son going to college and suddenly even his younger sister, a high school sophomore, turned her thoughts to college. The family learned that his room and board would be funded by a work-study program, which Steven eagerly accepted. His first semester was challenging but Steven was able to maintain a 3.0 GPA and learned how to study in a noisy dorm by using headphones. By his senior year, still living in the dorm, he decided to take out a small student loan to help pay for an apartment so that he could concentrate on his studies. He is now teaching in his old high school, side by side with the AP teacher who believed in him, while he attends graduate school at night.

Steven's advice to high school seniors?

Believe, always believe, that if you have the grades, the motivation, and the drive, that there are people to help you get there, no matter what. I would have never dreamed that I would have a degree from Baylor University, but I do. All you have to do is work really hard, decide what you want, and the path will just open up for you. Tell the admissions people about your struggles, your dreams, your vision and they will get to know you. Get people that know you best to write recommendations for you that describe things you did with them and for them. That really counts. Then, study for the tests and practice writing the essay until you can do it in your sleep. Get people to help you edit it and give you some constructive ideas on your writing style. Listen to them and express yourself.

The Committed (Well, Almost): Gina

Drill team member, student council officer, office assistant, and summer worker at her stepfather's dental office were just a few activities that Gina wrote down on her application to Texas Christian University. Coming from an affluent family, she had a college fund that would pay for the tuition to a private school. Combined, her SAT scores were 1025 and she had excellent recommendations from teachers who had known her since fourth grade. Her volunteer activities as a youth-group leader and church nursery volunteer were impressive. Her grade point average was 3.0. She worked hard to get good grades but always found school challenging. She avoided Advanced Placement classes, afraid of the reading assignments, and instead took two college classes for dual credit at a local junior college, approved by her high school, while still a senior.

Gina's mother had attended Texas Christian University and was heralding her daughter's future in her own sorority there. Gina admired her mother, particularly since she had reared her younger sister and her as a single parent after her father died. Because of her admiration, she chose to write about her mother for her college essay, the topic of which was "Discuss a significant person, experience, or achievement that has special meaning to you." Gina was private about her essay so she did not show it to anyone, even for editing. While Gina's essay was full of emotion and admiration for her mother, she forgot to say how her mother's strength had a special meaning in her own life. The admissions officer noted that on her rejection letter.

After being placed on the wait list due to her GPA and poor essay, Gina sat back and waited until TCU eventually admitted her in May of her senior year, partially due to a spot that opened up when another student declined admission. Gina pledged her mother's sorority the first semester, which filled her time with sorority life, late night dates, and little studying. Soon the failure notices went out and Gina realized she had gotten into more than she had bargained for. She begged her parents for a transfer to a smaller state school and eventually won the debate. She graduated four years later with a good GPA and the satisfaction that she had done it "her way."

When Gina was asked for her advice to give to high school seniors reading this book, she said:

Think about why you are going to college and choose one that fits you. That can be hard if your parents think differently, but just talk to them . . . and let them know that you just want to try it on your own. Use words that describe your real self and your motivation to succeed. And when you write your essay, use phrases that describe who you admire, how they helped you, and who you want to be someday. The essay is about you and it is the only way the admissions committee will get to know you. Remember that everything you write down on your application is in competition with everyone else's application so it really has to stand out. Finally, you have to be committed to the school you go to or else you won't study. It has to fit you.

The Honest: Sean

When I met Sean in his junior year as his high school counselor, he immediately impressed me with his drive to become a veterinarian: "Dr. Metcalf, tell me who your dog's vet is. I want to interview him for my English paper. Did I tell you that I want to be a vet? I plan on going to Texas A&M, the best vet school in the country. I work for a vet, Dr. Smith, after school until about nine o'clock each night. Do you think he will give me a good recommendation? Who else should I ask? Do you know anything about scholarships for kids like me?"

Kids like him. Yes, there are lots of scholarships for a straight-A student who had worked for the veterinarian Dr. Smith, for two years, who was involved in the Future Farmers of America since he was able to join as a freshman, and had taken every AP science and math class available. With a fee waiver for his SAT, he made a combined score of 1430. He was poor, but only financially. He was rich in intelligence and drive. He came from a family where his father, a farmer, barely made ends meet and his mother, a school secretary, sold tickets at the football games for extra cash. Yes, I knew of scholarships for kids like him. He just had to compose an essay that exposed the kid he was.

He did. He wrote the essay about growing up poor and helping his father out on the farm early in the morning before going to school. He wrote about how he fell in love with animals as a very young boy when he saw the birth of a calf and how he loved taking care of all the animals on the farm all of his life. He wrote about feeling like an outcast when his clothes weren't designer brands when he got to high school and then he wrote about how he came to realize that the clothes didn't matter. It was the man inside the person who mattered. A man he admired became the subject of his essay, too, and that was his father. His father's father had come from Germany and began a life here with his grandmother. He struggled, but had four sons that he always encouraged to do their best. In his eyes, they did. In Sean's eyes, his father did the same, always encouraging him to study so he could become the veterinarian that he wanted to be. His father, Sean said in his essay, taught him about strength, resiliency, God, values, and family ties. He took all of those values with him to Texas A&M University. Today he attends the Texas A&M School of Veterinary Medicine.

Sean's advice:

You might not have the best clothes or the best car but if you have a dream, you have everything. Think about that dream every day and it

*will come true. I promise it will. I didn't have a family that could afford
to send me to college but I didn't let that stop me. If you know what you
want to do, get someone at school to help you find a way to do it. Write
an essay that tells your story so the admissions people know who you
are. Put your dreams on paper. Let God do the rest.*

All of these stories convey the importance of communicating who you are
and what your goals and dreams are as you jump over the hurdles of getting
into college. Each story portrays what schools are looking for in applicants. In
Gina's case, she knew that TCU had high academic standards and that she
would be in competition with other students whose grades were better than
hers, yet she neglected to use words that would send a clear message that she
was just as committed as the others. She also chose the wrong college by listening to her parents and not voicing her own needs. This lessened her commitment and resulted in her transfer. In Steven's case, being committed and
responsible at his job led him to capitalize on his experiences with words that
emphasized his obvious writing capabilities. His essay was one that the admissions director described as "one of the best we have received in years." His
commitment to succeed was rewarded with a diploma.

And Sean, full of promise and hope but limited in resources—his honesty
about his challenging and demanding surroundings made his application glow
with possibilities. *"You are the kind of student that we award full scholarships
to at Texas A&M,"* the admissions director wrote. Sean's honest approach to
stating how he desperately needed a scholarship or grant to fund his education
due to his parent's inability to qualify for any loan or provide any sort of financial support gained the interest of the admissions team. Along with his
superior grades, excellent recommendations from his FFA teacher and Dr.
Smith, high SAT scores, and an essay that conveyed his true voice, Sean was
able to capture a place at the college of his dreams. A work-study program
gave him extra money for college events and was a cinch for him to combine
with studying. He had, after all, proven that he could handle quite a lot at his
young age already.

Qualifications That Colleges Crave

So, it's time for you to apply, along with the brightest, the most committed, and the most honest high school students everywhere. From among the 17 million that will apply this year, how will you get the initial attention of the admissions staff? The following summary was taken from a wide variety of responses from colleges and university admission staff that I interviewed across the country:

The University of Oregon
Harvard University
Brown University
Texas Christian University
Texas Wesleyan University
Boston University
Southern Methodist University
The University of Southern California
Texas Woman's University
The United States Military Academy
The University of Florida
Baylor University
The University of Texas
Purdue University
The University of Michigan

In addition, school counseling students, working on their master's degree at Texas Woman's University, did research on college applications and provided me with a wealth of information that I have passed along here. Read and take notice, then let them guide you to the college finish line.

1. A high school transcript that includes the most rigorous courses available.

Since you are going to college, it's time to review the meaning of the word "rigorous" in regard to how colleges interpret it. The word itself refers to courses requiring *great or extreme bodily, mental, or spiritual strength*— courses such as AP (Advanced Placement) or IB (International Baccalaureate) or any other honors courses that push and prod your thinking and require extra reading. These are *rigorous* courses, as are classes that you can take at a community or local college for dual credit (you get both high school and college credit) while still in high school. Any other *rigorous* courses that you can elect to take instead of choosing senior release time, where you might get the afternoon off, count big with the admissions team. These courses often add extra points to your GPA, which is then referred to as *"weighted."*

You should also take more courses than you *need* for high school graduation. For example, if you are thinking of pursuing an art degree, and have taken Art 1, Art 2, and Art 3, take more courses related to Art such as Photography and sign up to work on the school newspaper after school. Ask yourself a question such as: "What other courses might prepare me better for becoming a premed major?" Then, take every advanced or honors science class that is available, plus extra math courses. If you are looking toward political science as a major, take the required history, government, and economics courses, plus psychology and sociology. And don't fret if your high school doesn't offer AP or IB classes. According to the University of Oregon, most colleges will understand if your small high school doesn't give you access to AP and IB classes. They will still give you points when you take any of the additional courses mentioned above, particularly if some of them are labeled "honors." Taking the most challenging courses in your high school will give you reasons to describe yourself on your application or in your essay with words such as the following:

HOW TO SAY IT

motivated	*decisive*	*enthusiastic*
determined	*resolute*	*ambitious*
driven		

These words describe a student who will add to class discussions. Every college interviewed mentioned that they aspired to add such students to their campus so that they could contribute to a rich environment. They want you to be an interesting and fascinating student who wants to learn.

2. Grades that show effort and academic growth during high school years, even if there were hard times.

Remember your freshman year in high school? You learned, sometimes by default, that everything counted, and you soon learned that not turning in some homework assignments could turn a 100 on every test into a final grade of C or worse. The freshman year in college will also be an eye-opener. It will be up to you to study on your own without your parents pushing you, and you will rarely be told to finish assignments by your professors. Instead, you will most likely be given a syllabus (a calendar of requirements) for the class that is often set in stone without exceptions. Because of this expected independence, when colleges see that your grades have consistently improved or stayed steadily in the above-average range in high school, they will be confident that you can be successful in college. That also means that during the last semester of your senior year, when prom and award ceremonies fill your calendar and you have parties to attend, you still study. Maintain the grades that the college sees on your application. They can and will actually tell you to unpack your things if your final transcript falls way below what your application transcript led them to believe about you. Keep the faith. Keep the grades up to the end.

A word here, too, about any hardships that you might have overcome during high school. If you moved, experienced the loss of a family member, had an accident, became ill, or had something happen that interfered with your academic performance, mention it in your application. Most applications ask for this kind of information. Describe your situation as honestly and sincerely as you can. Perhaps phrases such as the following might fit with what you went through:

HOW TO SAY IT

Developed a new understanding due to . . .
Gained insight through my experiences that . . .
Developed skills that helped me to deal . . .
Encountered new emotions when . . .
Gained a know-how that helped me to . . .
Learned that I could handle . . .
It was difficult getting through the accident, but I did by . . .

3. Solid scores on standardized tests that are consistent or higher than the high school transcript and rank.

The scores that you receive on college aptitude tests should be consistent with your high school performance. Sometimes, however, students make higher scores on the standardized tests than high school work. Since today's colleges look at the entire student, scoring high on the aptitude tests while maintaining a B average is a plus. Colleges are interested in the intriguing student that shows improvement.

There are vast numbers of students who fall a bit below our academic profile but are tenacious and persistent and well-prepared to succeed. We want to be sure they're at our table, too," says Karen Foust, vice president for enrollment at Hendrix College in Arkansas, which, like all of the college-counselor favorites mentioned in this piece, fares quite respectably in U.S. News*'s rankings. Some thirty percent of last year's freshman class arrived with grade-point averages between*

2.5 and 3.5. Adds Scott Friedhoff, vice president for enrollment at Allegheny College in Pennsylvania: "I can think of any number of us who would be glad to accept most of our strong B applicants with combined verbal and math SAT scores of 1150. (McGrath, A., America's Best Colleges, U.S. News & World Report 2006 Edition, *p. 10)*

Most schools on the East and West Coasts prefer the SAT, while the *ACT* is the test of choice in the Midwest. However, check with your school of choice to see which they prefer. During your junior year, take the *PSAT*, as it gives a fairly accurate view of how you will do on the SAT and will show you where to study up on your skills for the test. Chapter 3 will give you pointers on how to score well on the SAT and ACT. The important thing to remember is to take either test over and over until you get the score that you think is your best. The SAT will show all of your scores on the report sheet while the ACT will not.

If you are a straight-A student, your SAT score should hover between 1450–1580. If you are a B student, your scores should be in the 1100–1200 range. If your grades are in the low Bs and you score in the 1100–1300 range, high ranking colleges will still give you some serious consideration. Never give up.

4. A passionate involvement in extracurricular and curricular activities that demonstrates leadership and determination to make a difference in the world.

When interviewed, the University of Southern California admissions officer said that USC is determined to attract the most diverse students to their campus. In this case, diversity means students that are well rounded and interested in a lot of things such as engineering, psychology, math, and music and are willing to study them all as a student at USC. At Texas Christian University in Fort Worth, Texas, an admissions officer relayed the importance of listing those *extracurricular activities* in the *order of importance to the student*. The officer said that sometimes after reading four or five descriptions of extra-curricular activities, they go on to look at the rest of the application, so make sure that you list your top five first.

TCU also said that its admissions staff looks for the student that has been involved in theater since the seventh grade, not only as an actor but as someone involved with writing, lighting, and set design. And, if that student carried through with the theater interests throughout high school consistently, and was in a leadership position, they become intriguing to TCU as a potential admission.

5. Participation in community services that show concern about one's city or interests that are heartfelt.

It's easy for most teens to sleep in on a Saturday morning, but if you are a teen that has become involved in local community interests such as the animal shelter, homeless shelter, or church-centered work for those less fortunate than yourself, it is vital that you put those items down in order of importance and explain what *being involved* did for you as a person. Doing so shows integrity, determination, and motivation to make a difference.

Mention, too, how working in the area brought you satisfaction and made you more determined than ever to work hard for a cause or a cure. Perhaps a family member died of cancer and you chose to participate in the Susan G. Komen Race for the Cure each year with your mother. This may become a topic for your essay that involves citing how someone made a difference in your life. If you choose to write on that subject, spend the first paragraph writing about the person and the rest of the essay writing about how it impacted you, your feelings, your future, and your actions. To cite one admissions director, it is "depth, not breadth of experience that counts." Phrases that might get you started are listed next.

HOW TO SAY IT

When this event happened to me, it made me . . .

I noticed that there were others less fortunate than me and it made me . . .

There had to be something I could do . . .
I felt as if I needed to . . .
I thought about how I could make a difference . . .
I knew I had to do something when . . .

6. Employment that shows a good work ethic or volunteer activities that illustrate responsibility and reliability to others and a commitment to follow through.

By now, hopefully you have been employed during the summer or have volunteered in community- or church-related situations so that people associate you with that position. Colleges look at employment records as a historical view of how you follow through responsibly and get along with those in authority. When the time comes for recommendations, choose the boss that you worked for the longest and the most successfully that you feel would describe you as:

hardworking	*likeable*	*team player*
trustworthy	*good with people*	*responsible*
dependable	*leader*	

A job or other meaningful use of free time can demonstrate maturity, too. Maybe you volunteered at the local hospital or rode with an EMT occasionally to understand their job and help out. Perhaps you took care of your ill grandmother while your mother worked at night, earned money by mowing lawns all summer, or worked for your father's business each summer to help him out. These activities and employment situations show the kind of person that you are. Mention them with pride.

7. An honest essay that sounds as if it were written by an eighteen-year-old, showing insight and aspirations for the future.

Honestly, every admissions director and staff member that I spoke to said the same thing: *"We want the voice and personality of the student to come through in the essay . . . it needs to sound like an eighteen-year-old."* At TCU, the admissions officer said that there is "so much polishing that goes into the process of college applications that sometimes the student loses her voice. We want to hear the voice." What does this mean? It means that you should talk to the admission committee in your application. Describe your passion, your beliefs, your dreams, and your aspirations. Mention how someone was important to you and then elaborate, a lot, on how it impacted you and where you see yourself in the future. The essay that you write should help you shine through on paper, describing who you are. In chapter 7, we will get down to the basics of essay writing, but until then, begin thinking of what you want the admissions staff to know and to learn about you. This is a time to brag. Just brag honestly.

8. Unique letters of recommendation from teachers that describe your leadership, commitment, and willing participation in discussions.

In chapter 4, you will write a résumé from a template and fill out an Experience Worksheet that you can give to your favorite teachers, school counselors, church ministers, priests, coaches, supervisors, employers, and community leaders so that they can compose a letter of recommendation that describes you perfectly. Until then, think of classroom discussions that you were involved in during school and write down how you participated. Then, when you begin requesting recommendations, remind your teachers of those discussions and ask them to write down some factors about your involvement. Stay involved in those discussions, too, until you graduate, because in college, you will often be invited to speak out on issues in class or outside of class. High school doesn't end in January of your senior year. It ends with graduation. Practice makes perfect and it helps you gain confidence.

9. Organization and a sense of preparedness for college and all of the experiences ahead.

The admissions director at the University of Oregon said that the college application process is in itself an education. It is a lesson in planning, scheduling, submitting, receiving, returning phone calls, and getting applications to the right person at the right time and right place. While high school had its deadlines, colleges are not as flexible. Get a calendar and begin making plans now, as you read this book. Later in chapter 5 on applications, you will have a chance to look at the timeline for the college application process. Keep your calendar in a place where you can look at it to see what's next. If you don't like paper calendars, figure out how to use the calendar in your cellular phone, PC, or laptop. If you are a student that needs prodding by your parents, ask them to prompt you when a deadline nears. This is a time when you need support from those who have experienced deadlines and schedules. Take their help as just that, help, and not as pressure. The pressure happens only if you are remiss in doing what needs to be done. Stay on track. Think of how you have followed through with other deadlines in your high school life such as trying out for the team, or submitting an application for a play or community activity. Then, just do it.

10. A diverse student that is not only interested in one subject area but in many subject areas and is willing to study them all.

If you live in a large city, chances are that you have been exposed to music, theater, sports, historical monuments, and a multitude of interesting activities. If you live in a small town, chances are that you have been exposed to other kinds of activities such as agricultural or industrial business. No matter where you come from, perhaps there are things that you would like to know more about. List your interests and curiosities in the application so that the reader recognizes your desire to learn. Most college admissions staff said that they were interested in the "well-rounded student" who pursued academics and outside activities, but they also wanted students to be interested in learning about a wide range of subjects. Think about it . . . by doing this, the college campus is more than a place for the smart kids. It becomes a place where smart kids meet interesting kids and together make for a fascinating experience. So, as you compile your résumé in the chapter on applications, include the honors and awards that you have received plus your unusual or unique talent or experiences, or anything else that makes you stand out. This is a time in your life where you should brag, brag, brag.

Quiz: Who Me?

So, who are you? Are you among the brightest students in your school, or the most committed to a cause or school project? Are you honest and value honesty in others? Have you put your best foot forward and studied hard, achieving a good GPA that you are proud of? Are you ready to put yourself out there and speak to the admissions staff in your voice about what it means to you to attend their college or university? Are you ready to write about someone that impressed you and made a difference in your life? Do you have experiences that have inhibited you from living like other students and have challenged you throughout high school, yet, you still made it? Are you eager to learn about a variety of subjects in addition to one that you are passionate about? And how about your test scores . . . are you satisfied? Or, are you willing to take them again and again to achieve what you know you are capable of?

This quiz is easy to grade. If you answered "yes" to any one of these questions, you are a student that is ready to apply to college. You are ready to race with the brightest, the most committed, and the most honest students of the world toward your slot on the freshman list of the college of your choice. Before you go, take a look at the first College Trivia Quiz to check out where some

College Trivia Quiz #1

What college, formerly a women's college but now coeducational, graduated actresses Téa Leoni (*Bad Boys, Jurassic Park III, The Family Man*) and Lisa Kudrow (*Friends, Romy and Michelle's High School Reunion*)?

a) Oberlin College
b) Vassar College
c) Hunter College
d) Radcliffe College
e) Goucher College

of your favorite celebrities went to school. You will find the answers in the appendix under College Trivia Quiz Answers.

Last, here is one of the unique parts of this book. In addition to getting all that you need to know to get into college, you get the College Clues and Cues in each chapter. Each clue and cue is designed to give you some tips on how to get things rolling for college, stay in college, and survive during the challenges. And, I've added some clues for your parents, too, who, you may feel at times, are truly clueless about the process. You see, this is not just a time for you to leave home; it's a time for your parents to let go. So, I've included College Clues and Cues for Parents so they can learn new ways to help you to leave home with confidence and support. Show it to them so that your last few months together are good ones for both of you.

College Clues and Cues

Colleges want you to be successful. They want you to finish the coursework and graduate with the best experience of your life. That's why they chose you, the very best student with the best experiences. They also want you to appear flexible and motivated to learn and contribute the most to their college campus. One college admissions director told me that getting in your applications or test scores *on time* meant that you were organized and prepared for college. He said that students who respond to requests to get additional parts of the application, such as transcripts or letters of recommendations, in on time impress them. It also means you can handle the stress of their college and will graduate from there. *That* is the goal of the college you pick—to make you an alumni. Impress them with your promptness, starting today. Ladies and gentlemen, get your calendars ready! Ask yourself these key questions to stay on track:

> *How have I gotten other assignments in on time during my high school years?*

> *How did I make other deadlines such as applications for Key Club or student council activities?*

> *What can my parent(s) do to help me get things in on time? When is a good time to ask them for help so that they listen?*

HOW TO SAY IT

Try using words like these to get the help from your parents (or older siblings, if they have gone to college and your parents aren't available) when you need it. And do let them help you: Most parents like helping; it makes them feel important to you.

"Mom, I don't understand some things on the Common Application. Can you tell me a time tonight when you can help me?"

"Dad, I have to choose from one of these essay topics and they all sound good but I don't know which one to choose. When can you look them over with me?"

"I feel so frustrated. I have homework to do, practice to get to later tonight, and an essay to write. I know I can get it done but I don't know where to start. What do you do when you get frustrated like this?"

College Clues and Cues
For Parents

According to the admissions director at Boston University, your parenting isn't over "till it's over," and I'm not sure it's even over then! To help your future scholar to make the deadlines and turn in the required documents, encourage your student to get a calendar and help her to fill it in, using the timeline in chapter 4. If your son or daughter prefers to program the information into their cell phone, let them. This is the preferred way that students today keep on top of their appointments and deadlines. If you meet resistance, remember that you have at least three times more life experience (sorry to remind you) than your offspring, who doesn't realize that colleges have deadlines and are not always flexible. Most colleges and universities have application deadlines and they do cut off applications at that time.

One college admission director said, "Applying to college should be in itself an educational experience." Using this advice, think of how you have motivated your son or daughter before and use those tactics during this time to help him get direction and meet deadlines. And, if you notice that your son or daughter is reluctant to fill out a particular application, talk about it. Maybe it's not a college that he is interested in. Be ready to be disappointed if your alma mater isn't your daughter's choice. Instead, see that difference of opinion as evidence of your child's growth and independence. As a parent, that should be your ultimate goal When you walk into the room to talk about these issues, ask yourself, "What do I hope to accomplish and how can I accomplish it best?"

HOW TO SAY IT

The words below might come in handy if you find yourself pacing back and forth as the deadline approaches:

"Sarah, remember last year when you were in cheerleading and taking two AP classes, yet somehow you managed to do gymnastics three times a week in addition to staying on the honor roll? I was so impressed with you. You were so committed and organized. Tell me how you did that?" (Wait for smiles and answers.)

Then:

"During the next four months, you have the SAT to take and college applications to request. Tell me how you think you can approach this so that the deadlines are made. I have them here. Let's look at them together." (Wait for answers.)

Then:

"If you get busy, tell me how I can remind you about the deadlines in a way that you will listen to carefully. I know how much you have to do." (Wait for answers.)

Finally:

"What else can I do to help you during this busy time? You are important to me and this is a special time for both of us. It matters to me that things go well for you." (Wait for answers.)

This approach helps your son or daughter to feel empowered because you are not telling your future college scholar what to do. You are looking back, recognizing their strengths in other situations, and tacking them on to the current situation as solutions. Additionally, asking what *you* can do will save you from hearing, "Dad, you're nagging me . . . I can do it myself," as the door slams. You don't want the last year that you have together to be filled with quarreling. Instead, make it a time when you help the future adult in your house to learn that there are deadlines that must be met, in a way that you might approach a colleague. This will keep the peace in your house and get things done.

2

You're Moving Out,
But *Where* Are You Going?

*"Cheshire Puss," she began, rather timidly, as she did not
at all know whether it would like the name . . . "Would you tell me,
please, which way I ought to go from here?" "That depends a good deal
on where you want to get to," said the Cat. "I don't much
care where—" said Alice. "Then it doesn't matter which
way you go," said the Cat.*

—Lewis Carroll, Alice's Adventures in Wonderland

The temperature in January 2005 dropped to 1 degree Fahrenheit at the Boston University campus. At Purdue, in West Lafayette, Indiana, it is sometimes so cold during December that most students opt for a microwave dinner versus going out for pizza. And of course, at the University of Texas, in September, the temperature was still hovering around 100 degrees Fahrenheit. While weather might not seem to be a crucial decision maker (unless you have your eye on the University of Hawaii), it is one of many that must be considered as you think of where you are going to school. How big is the campus? What are the dormitories like? How many majors are there and what is required to be accepted into the department? Are there fraternities and sororities? Is there a religious affiliation? What is the policy on *hazing*? Is it safe? Is it too far from home? Is it far enough from home? How much does it cost and is there enough financial aid to attend?

Hopefully, unlike Alice, you probably *do* care which way you're going and you're ready to follow the Cheshire Cat's suggestion of figuring out which way that will be. You're ready to pack and ready to meet new people. You can't wait to get out from under your parent's "guidance" and experience college. But exactly where are you going to college and how will you make that decision anyway? Maybe by now some of your close high school friends have made plans to room together, yet you're thinking that their college choice might not work for you. Maybe you've decided to step out on your own and attend a large state university 100 miles away. Good for you. Yet, you wonder how you would fare in classes of more than 100 students in a school of 50,000 students. If your high school was small and you enjoyed knowing each of your classmates, a large school would take some adapting to. But, if the state school is only 100 miles away, that's also close enough to come home and do laundry occasionally yet far enough away so that your parents won't visit too much. It's a big decision. To help you begin thinking about what you are looking for, answer the following question. It is called the Miracle Question. It is a goal-setting question that will help you to step into the future and imagine what you need and desire from the college of your choice. It is designed to help you understand what you want to accomplish and need to study to be successful over the next four years of your life.

Suppose tonight while you sleep, a miracle happens. You wake up tomorrow and, because of the miracle, you are attending the college of your dreams. It is exactly what you had hoped for and you feel successful at what you are doing.

Thinking about that day, where would you be?

What would you be doing?

Who would be there?

What else would be going on that would tell you that this was the best college ever for you?

The answers to this question are important as they will give you insight into what the most important aspects of the right college are for you. With these answers, the rest of this chapter will help you to focus on what it will take to begin achieving your "miracle." First, let's do a checklist to see what's important to you and rate them so that you know what the most important aspects of a college are to *you* right now.

The Miracle College Survey

Look through the following checklist and rate the following items. Rate the *extremely important* ones a "1" and the *important* ones a "2." If it's not that important to you, rate it a "3."

1. ———— types of degrees offered
2. ———— interesting majors/minors
3. ———— location (is it in a rural or urban setting)/distance from home
4. ———— size of the college or university
5. ———— public universities vs. private colleges
6. ———— costs: tuition and financial assistance packages (scholarships available)
7. ———— campus resources (labs, libraries, computer access, equipment)
8. ———— internships/study abroad
9. ———— faculty qualifications
10. ———— school reputation/tier rank
11. ———— safety (campus, community)
12. ———— student body (diversity, gender, etc.)
13. ———— social life (Greek organizations, professional clubs)
14. ———— housing options (dorms, apartments, living at home)
15. ———— extracurricular activities (sports, volunteer organizations)

Now that you've done an inventory of what's important, read a bit more on each of the items that you checked off with "1s" and "2s" for more explanations. The numbers on the checklist correspond to the numbers on the items that follow next.

1. Types of degrees offered

As you look through the websites of the colleges that you are interested in, you may notice that there are different kinds of degrees offered by colleges that depend on a few factors. First, there are two-year or *associate's degrees* that community (junior) colleges award students. Most community colleges also offer certificates in a specialized field of training. Usually, students that begin their college studies at a community college go on to finish up at a four-year or senior college or university and get a *bachelor's degree,* unless they are able to get a certification in a skill at the community college.

If you dream of being a psychologist, school administrator, CEO of a huge company, or other high-level position someday, you may consider getting your *master's degree* or *doctoral degree.* If you aspire to be a doctor, dentist, or lawyer, you will be pursuing medical, dental, or law school, which all require prerequisite courses before you can apply. Tell your college advisor your plans and he/she will construct a *degree plan* to get you there.

2. Interesting majors/minors

When it comes to looking at majors, get ready . . . there are over 300 college majors to choose from. And, each school has many majors that they are well respected for. For example, at the University of Michigan's Taubman College of Architecture students learn how to design buildings around human beings and learn how to process what is needed for an aesthetically pleasing yet practical environment. At Drexel University's College of Media and Design, you can choose from majors in Film and Video, Graphic Design, Digital Media, Dramatic Writing, Photography, Fashion Design, Interior Design, and Design and Merchandising, as well as graduate programs (master's degrees) in Interior and Fashion Design. The University of Nebraska, like many state universities, has a branch campus in Omaha where students can study architectural, civil, computer, and electronics and construction engineering.

So, choosing a major means asking yourself *more* questions. Copy the next page, or write down your answers directly on the Interest Checklist page to sort out your interests and ideas about jobs and careers. The answers will give you clues regarding which college major suits you best.

Interest Checklist

What are my interests?

_____

_____

What did I learn about myself in high school that tells me I have a talent in a particular area?

_____

_____

What would some of my high school teachers encourage me to check out as a major?

_____

_____

Are there careers that I have always been interested in? If so, do those careers involve graduate school and am I willing to go to school for three to four more years after college?

_____

_____

Out of all these things listed, which would I like to do every day, as a job?

_____

_____

Are you one of those lucky individuals who has so many interests that it's hard to name just one? Can you be "undecided"? Sure, you can, but only for the first year. At Waynesburg College, the faculty actually voted to have students delay the declaration of a major until at least the end of the first year because they wanted the students to have opportunities to explore the many options available to them. But, at the end of that year, a major has to be declared. Most colleges and universities interviewed for this book were in agreement with Waynesburg on this issue. The best information, however, will come from your college advisor, whom we will discuss later in this book.

Either way, choosing a college that's right for you means choosing one that has a variety of majors that interest you. That way, at the end of the first year, you can "name that major" with ease and confidence.

HOW TO SAY IT

While you are thinking about a major, write or e-mail the colleges that you are interested in (choose at least six of them . . . more on that in chapter 4 and write a brief note like the one that follows:

Dear Possible College of My Choice,

My name is Susie Senior and I will graduate from Best High School in May 2007. I am interested in pursuing a bachelor's degree in Communications. Would you please send me information on that major and any other information regarding the kinds of positions that your graduates have obtained after receiving that degree from your university?

My e-mail is susies@yol.com and my physical address is:

Susie Senior
1234 Scenic Avenue
Success City, Nevada 56789

Thank you,
Susie Senior

To write a note such as this one, you will need to look over a few of the many majors out there for you to choose from, as presented by the College Board, the folks that produce the SAT. When you write or e-mail the colleges that you are interested in attending, use these words to describe the majors that you are interested in. You can also check out what each major involves by going to www.collegeboard.com and clicking on the major.

Architecture and Natural Resources
Architecture and Environmental Design
Arts: Visual and Performing
Biological (Life) Science
Business and Commerce
Communications
Computer and Information Sciences and Technologies
Education
Engineering and Engineering Technologies
Foreign and Classical Languages
General and Interdisciplinary Studies
Health Professions and Allied Services
Home Economics
Language and Literature
Library and Archival Sciences
Mathematics
Military Sciences
Philosophy, Religion, and Theology
Physical Sciences
Public Affairs and Services
Social Science and History, General
Technical and Vocational
Undecided
(www.collegeboard.com, 2006)

3. Location (is it in a rural or urban setting)/distance from home

When our oldest son, Roger, was admitted to Boston University, he went to visit the campus. He liked the people, the campus, and the majors but realized that living 1,750 miles away from home was not what he was ready for. He eventually opted to attend Baylor University that fall for his bachelor's degree, which was 100 miles away. Later, after graduation, he moved to Boston to attend graduate school.

Our youngest son, Ryan, originally attended the University of North Texas, fifty miles away. He told me how his roommate of Chinese decent, from Hawaii, was startled one morning when he woke up to see snow for the first time. It doesn't snow that often in Texas and it wasn't as deep as the snow in Minnesota, but his roommate was very excited. He had hoped to have a different college experience and that was the first of many.

The fact is, choosing a location for college is sometimes underestimated. It can make the difference between feeling comfortable enough to concentrate on studying and feeling so homesick or left out of activities that you end up transferring closer to home the next semester. It helps to check things out by visiting the campus, reading campus newspapers, and talking to students on campus. And, of course, asking yourself some more questions so you can prevent a few mishaps. Check these out:

Do you feel drawn to a big city? Why?

Are you drawn to a small town or wilderness for a secluded environment? Why?

Are you more comfortable in a familiar place or do you want to branch out?

Are you interested in meeting new kinds of people in new surroundings?

Do you prefer a campus with a strong religious presence?

Make lots of visits or, if you can't visit, contact the college and ask an admissions staff person to have a student call you or e-mail you about their experiences. Remember, along with learning academics, your experience at college is meant to teach you much more. Make that experience available and no matter where you go, you won't be disappointed.

4. Size of the college or university

Let's say you come from a small town and you're ready to get some new experiences and move uptown. You choose to apply to your state university with more than 50,000 students. What can you expect to find when you visit or show up in August?

> *A huge variety of majors, courses, and degrees*
> *Large class sizes*
> *Huge and complete libraries*
> *Many housing opportunities, including sorority and fraternity houses*
> *Many social opportunities, clubs, and organizations*
> *Well-funded sports programs and marching band*
> *Some famous faculty members with research interests*
> *Courses taught by teaching assistants sometimes, not professors, who are doing research*
> *Less teacher-student interaction*
> *A possible feeling of being lost in a crowd*
> *Great school spirit and community involvement*

Then there is the smaller college, with a gender preference or religious affiliation. There, you might find the following:

> *Individual and personal advising system*
> *Fewer majors to choose from, some affiliated with the college's preference and focus*

Smaller class sizes

Professors teach courses and have more time to interact personally with students

Professors know their students' names when they see them on campus

Community supports the college and provides volunteer services

Fewer resources and less equipment

Good opportunities to "know everyone"

Smaller libraries

Less entertainment locally

Fewer social opportunities such as fewer sororities and fraternities

Less emphasis on sports programs

Some of you may find sitting in a class of 300 students exciting while others will prefer to know that their professor knows their name. Think about what makes you the most comfortable. If you were a go-getter in high school, there's a good chance that you will do the same at a large university and find your niche. If you were more of the average Joe in high school, socially, then the smaller school might be your ticket to feeling comfortable enough to study and make all of those As. Again, visit the school and get a feel for school spirit, friendliness, and excitement. Or, if you want to really check things out, write the following note or e-mail your inquiry to find out more about what's unique about the small or large campus:

HOW TO SAY IT

Dear Small or Large Campus,

I am a high school senior at Best High School and am beginning to explore which colleges to apply to for a major in Education. I am debating whether to choose to attend a small or large university. Could you please send me information on campus life and class size? My e-mail is susies@yol.com and my physical address is:

Susie Senior
1234 Scenic Avenue
Success City, Nevada 56789

Thank you,
Susie Senior

5. Public universities vs. private colleges

As a high school counselor, I often heard from parents of gifted seniors that they were discouraging their offspring from applying to private colleges or universities because "they couldn't afford them." While their economic status was behind their words, they were often misinformed about the realities of private costs versus public costs. The fact is that up to 40 percent of the students at private colleges are on scholarships when they qualify for them. Qualifying is not too difficult either. There are scholarships for academic excellence and need.

The more important facts to consider are the types of majors, location, prestige, and opportunities. There may also be religious affiliations that you are drawn to that support your values. These are important considerations. And don't forget the prestige and reputation part, particularly if you see yourself going on for a master's degree or doctorate.

So, to summarize, it will serve you well to apply to both. Choose several private colleges and universities as well as several state colleges and universities and send off those applications. Choose those that have the majors that you are interested in and are known for certain kinds of graduates. For example, back in the dark ages when I applied for my first job as a middle school teacher, the recruiter from Arlington Independent School District came to the Baylor University campus just to recruit teachers. "Baylor teachers are among the best," I remember him saying to me, so they chose to visit there each spring and hired not only me but many of my friends. Knowing how the degrees from a particular university are viewed by the community in which you plan on working will guide you toward which schools to apply to. For example, we all know that graduates of Harvard Law School are viewed with a bit more esteem than other law schools. And since President George Bush graduated from Yale, that university carries quite a bit of clout, too. Think about what institution you want to be associated with for the rest of your life and how that association will help you to succeed. Long after you are married, have kids, and are moving up in your career, where you attended college will still come up in conversation. Choose a college or university that you are proud to represent.

6. Costs: tuition and financial assistance packages (scholarships available)

Your parents will probably be looking at this item more than you but it is important that you also understand tuition costs, housing, and meal plans. In chapter 4 we will touch on financial aid strategies for paying for college. Here, though, if money is an item that will make or break your decision, it's important to review some basics.

First and foremost, try to *not let* money stand in the way at first of your decision on which colleges and universities to apply to. I know that sounds as if I believe everyone has had a college fund since they were two days old, but the reality is, if the private college or university of your dreams accepts your application, sends you a welcome letter, and really wants you to attend, the financial aid department *will help you* search for the money to go there. That's their job. Some have even been known to bargain with students that were accepted at other universities that gave them a better financial aid package. That can mean that what a private university ends up costing after you are awarded grants and scholarships can be comparable to paying what a state university can cost without a scholarship. That can open many more doors to you. And, if a state university offers you a scholarship as well, then your choices just broadened and you are in the driver's seat.

There is also a difference between in-state tuition and out-of-state tuition. In-state tuition is lower because it means that since you and your parents live in that state, they pay taxes that go to public universities in that state. If you choose a state university outside of your own state, you pay tuition comparable to a private university because your parents don't pay taxes in that state. There are still scholarships and grants as well as loans to repay for college at either place.

7. Campus resources (labs, libraries, computer access, equipment)

When I attended college, I went to the library to check out books. Today, when I go to my university library where I work, I can view audio and visual media, request a book from a university in another state, get a librarian to send me journal articles through e-mail, and request to be a part of a distance-learning classroom. Wow.

Today in college and university libraries there is an array of media that include digital formats, such as audio compact disc and digital video disc (DVD), and interactive multimedia, such as CD-ROM and DVD-ROM. I can request media resources that can now be delivered via the Web, digital satellite systems, and a host of rapidly developing technologies. Double wow.

Depending on the size of your university, and its funding, of course, you may have access to advanced and new equipment for science study, computer technology, film/communications study, and much more, including the ability to check out equipment to take to your dorm or use on your class project. When my youngest son was thinking of transferring to Baylor University as a Telecommunications major, he visited the campus and learned of the many donations made by Sony. He also learned that each spring, certain students were chosen to attend the National Association of Broadcasters show in Las Vegas. He found the production department to be top-end and the postproduction editing equipment terrific. He transferred and on the first day of class was given a loan camera to make his first class project.

The moral of this story is: Check out the library, media services, internet access and find out what kind of equipment that you would be entitled to use. It may matter to you.

8. Internships/study abroad

It is very common in today's colleges for students in their junior or senior year to do *internships*, which are either paid or (mostly) unpaid opportunities to gain entry-level work experience in their major. Most internships are approved by the college and students gain college credits for them, since they pay tuition during the semester they are working at the internship. Each internship has a faculty supervisor that keeps in touch with the internship supervisor so that things work in the student's best interest. Often, those internships can turn into real jobs after graduation. If your college does not have an internship program, you can still do some hunting for one and then seek university approval after finding the right internship for you. Make sure to seek approval prior to beginning the internship so that you know the required number of hours (usually 100 to 150) that the university might require for credit.

The opportunity to study abroad for a semester or even an entire year is also offered at many universities. This is a wonderful chance for students to immerse themselves in a different culture and environment while taking courses that will still apply toward their degree. Imagine learning French while living in France eating croissants or studying art while living in Rome. Or, think of being a business major living in China for a semester and visiting a variety of successful businesses. These experiences are priceless and look great on résumés.

Check out the internship and study abroad programs at the colleges that you apply to. Do as many internships as you can during your junior and senior year as they prove your determination and give you experience that will help you get the job in the future. Talk to everyone you can at the internship site so that you can use them for references later. You are building a résumé for your future.

9. Faculty qualifications

Most students that apply to college have little knowledge of who their professors are or what they have studied to get to their positions, so here is a brief overview of who will be teaching you for the next four years.

Typically, two-year community colleges hire people with master's degrees to fill their full-time positions and teach at least three courses. There will also be professors in the community colleges with a doctorate, meaning that they earned a PhD or EdD and are to be addressed as "doctor." In addition, most two-year colleges expect their teachers to have teaching experience or experience with distance learning. They often work in the setting that they teach as an additional part-time job, such as a dental hygienist who teaches in a dental hygiene program.

Four-year colleges and universities almost always look for teachers, referred to as *professors* in various ranks: instructor, assistant, associate, and full professor with doctoral degrees. These positions are often referred to as *tenured*, which means that after a certain amount of years teaching, a professor can apply for increased rank, which gives him a guarantee of future employment. In some cases, instructors with a master's degree in areas of art, film, or photography may teach in a four-year college by possessing an impressive portfolio of work. Their work experience is considered comparable to that of a more advanced degree. So, always look for the credentials before addressing an instructor!

If you attend a small college or university, the chances are that you will be taught by the professor. If you attend a large college or university, you may be taught by a TA (teaching assistant). You may also be taught by an *adjunct professor*, who is often well qualified and hired when enrollment rises or a regular faculty member is working on a project.

A good way to find out about your future professors is to check out the college's website. These days it is common for faculty members to post a résumé online along with their research interests. Additionally, many faculty members have their own websites. Feel free to contact the faculty members with questions about their courses and their programs. Believe it or not, they welcome your inquiries!

10. *School reputation/tier rank*

In the same way that your senior class is ranked according to who achieves the highest grade point average (GPA), American colleges and universities are ranked once per year by *U.S. News & World Report* magazine. This is how they do it:

> *To rank colleges and universities,* U.S. News *first assigns schools to a group of their peers, based on categories developed by the Carnegie Foundation for the Advancement of Teaching. Those in the National Universities group are the 248 American universities (162 public and 86 private) that offer a wide range of undergraduate majors as well as master's and doctoral degrees; many strongly emphasize research.*
>
> *In each category, data on up to 15 indicators of academic quality are gathered from each school and tabulated. Schools are ranked within categories by their total weighted score. (www.usnews.com)*

Here is what the results look like:

Tier I schools include the Ivy League and other top-fifty colleges and universities, based upon factors that include, among other issues, such things as reputation, general and educational spending per student, annual giving by alumni, and standardized test score ranges.

Beyond the Ivy League there are **Tier II** schools that can make a difference for the right student, depending upon the needs, wants, values, and specific attributes an individual student holds as important during his or her college search. Tier II colleges number between 250 and 300, depending upon how a college chooses to be recognized by the Carnegie Foundation's classification system.

And what about the thousands of schools below Tier II? Attending one doesn't mean that you don't aspire to be president or to be the next great inventor. Among those who attend Tier III and IV schools, you'll find corporate, foundation, and civic leaders who entered college from a family and socioeconomic background different from yours or similar to yours. They graduated into a workforce with a specific set of skills, knowledge, and a vision of success shaped by very diverse experiences. These colleges and universities graduate individuals in a multitude of fields.

Check out www.usnews.com for listings of all of America's top colleges and other colleges that are value-priced but still offer valuable degrees.

11. Safety (campus, community)

At www.securityoncampus.org, you can obtain info on what to look for in your new home away from home. The *Family Educational Rights and Privacy Act (FERPA)* allows your parents and yourself to check out the safety measures covered by your future university.

HOW TO SAY IT

Call the colleges that you are interested in and ask to speak to someone about college safety. Say it like this:

> *"I am thinking of attending your college. Could you connect me with someone that could describe the safety and security measures that have been developed for students who live on campus?"*

> *"How would a student report a criminal incident?"*

> *"How is campus crime monitored?"*

> *"Do the dorms use electronic cards to enter the facility?"*

> *"What is the policy regarding guests, parents, and employees entering dormitories?"*

Everyone, including your parents and yourself, will sleep better knowing the safety measures that are being taken to ensure your best interest and safety. Let your parents know what you find out. It will not only ease their minds, it will make you look super responsible.

12. Student body (diversity, gender, etc.)

How many males? How many females? And what about diversity, not only in regard to culture and race, but in regard to geography and extracurricular and academic activities? Do you want to go to school with only brilliant academicians or with people that love photography *and* biology *and* skateboarding? Do you want to go to school with a homogenous group like your high school class back home, or, do you want a roommate from Scotland, Africa, or Australia? And how about involvement with the community so that you can learn who lives there? At the University of Notre Dame, 77 percent of their students are involved in service to their community. This not only spreads the goodwill of the university, it helps students see the value of being involved in a community.

HOW TO SAY IT

College is a time to stretch and learn about other kinds of people and other kinds of interests. Ask questions like these when you call or write about diversity:

What is the ratio between males and females?

What are some of the represented countries in your school in both faculty and students?

Are there organizations for international students as well as national students?

Does the college have an affirmative action policy?

13. Social life (Greek organizations, professional clubs)

Your college social life is a huge part of the transition from high school senior to young adult. How you approach getting started socially may depend on what is available to you. Many colleges allow freshmen to pledge a sorority or fraternity during the first semester. Think carefully about this temptation. You may be moving away from home, experiencing a new culture of instructors, and trying to study with a new face around (the roommate). Are you ready to schedule in the demands of being available for a club meeting and *pledging* several times a week? If you have always been vigilant in being organized and desire the social life as a means to feeling a part of college, go for it. But if you are slightly worried about making the grade while coping with the move and new environment, wait one semester. Learn about the different clubs and listen for the reputations of those clubs on campus. In this case, as in classwork, knowledge is the key.

> *When he arrived at Ohio State in 1995 as one of nearly 5,800 freshmen, Dave Diffendal felt lost. "I didn't have any friends," he recalls. "I was having a heck of a time meeting people." But the Pittsburgh native soon became a pledge of the Sigma Phi Epsilon fraternity and now, as a 19-year-old junior, he is chapter president . . . For Diffendal, Greek life has made a big university seem "a lot smaller." Jenny Nelson's experience as an Ohio State freshman was totally different. A self-styled Army brat who had attended three high schools, she felt at home on the Columbus campus the moment she arrived. At orientation, she listened skeptically as young women praised sorority life: "They said, 'It's a great social scene. You get T-shirts for being at parties.' I decided I could do without that" (Lord, 1997).*

Okay, yes, you are going to college to learn, but you are also going to go to college to do the following:

> *meet new people and immerse yourself in other cultures*
> *have fun*
> *grow intellectually and mentally through stimulating classes*
> *have fun*
> *experience freedom and make your own decisions*
> *have fun*

So, with these vital needs in mind, knowing the social life and climate of the university that you choose is essential. To accomplish this, the author contacted a successful college senior and asked her to provide you with some questions to ask of professors and students when you make your college visits.

An expert speaks

Ryan Weaver is a senior journalism major in the Honors Program at Emerson University in Boston, Massachusetts. She suggests the following tips when visiting a college and getting a glimpse of the college social scene and the social culture at the university:

Taking the tour of your prospective schools should not just include a glance at the library and a chat with the tour guide. Taking advantage of your time in town to do a little research on your own will be invaluable as you face what may be a tough decision between similar schools and majors.

To gauge the social scene at the university of your choice, during your campus visit, drive down fraternity row on weekend nights and stroll through the student hangouts. Are people behaving responsibly, or does the situation seem reckless and potentially dangerous? Do you see certain clubs on certain T-shirts or jerseys? If so, check them out by calling the sorority or fraternity house and talking to a member. Check, too, on the college website, and learn whether hazing is closely monitored. Even when students are injured across the country from hazing, it still happens. Stay safe.

Asking area students about your school and your major is a good way to get a ballpark idea of how your prospective choices stack up against others in the area. They most likely interact with each other in places ranging from the workplace to the subway, and can give you a peer-level idea. For example, if you are visiting several schools in the Boston area, you may ask students at Boston University to characterize their impressions of Boston College; if you are in Ithaca, ask Ithaca College students to talk about what their friends' lives at Cornell are like.

HOW TO SAY IT

Ask questions such as:

How much importance do students here place on prioritizing homework over fun?

What do people do for fun?	*Where do people go for:*
late-night food	*birthday parties*
pizza	*a nice dinner*
playing games	*outdoors activities*
social parties	

How much emphasis do students here place on drinking? Will I be comfortable if I don't like to drink?

Do people usually stay on campus or go off campus at night? What areas are popular?

Do students usually stay on campus or go home on the weekends?

How important is Greek life to the character of this school? What's the difference between professional and social fraternities/sororities? How will it benefit me to join one?

What other surrounding areas do people like to visit? How often can you get out of the campus area?

How much money will I need to have per week in order to have a good time here?

What is the sociological makeup here really like?

Will I feel comfortable here:
    If I am a religious or cultural minority?
    If I come from a different country?
    If my parents don't make much money?
    If English isn't my first language?

What other transportation options are open to me/how is public transportation here?

Do people here enjoy living in the dorms? Which is the best one? What makes it the best? (Proximity to classes and dining hall, safety, character of residents and residential directors.)

Do people here live in the dorms all four years, or move off campus? Why? How easy is it to obtain the kind of on-campus housing you want? What kinds of incentives does the college offer in order to house its residents? (Booking hotel rooms for students to live in for the year, offering grants for off-campus living, offering nicer rooms for upperclassmen.)

Do I need a car to live comfortably here? How many other students have one?

Ryan mentions the importance of speaking to students of different majors at the school that you are considering:

How do students perceive your major? How accepting are they of differences between them? For example, do they think that theater kids are "crazy," or that engineering students are "boring"? How difficult or easy do they consider your major in comparison with others?

How many professional clubs and organizations at this school are dedicated to my major? How do they compare to others at competing schools? How easy is it to join one and stay in one? How valuable will that experience be to my academic development?

Ryan also suggests asking some fact-finding questions like the ones that follow about classes and studying on campus. Students are especially helpful to ask because they will be able to give you more information on the vital supplementary experiences you might have at school, such as working for a college newspaper, joining a professional fraternity/sorority, or obtaining an internship. It's important, she mentions, to make sure not to overlook each school's offerings in these opportunities—there is more to learn at school than what is contained in the course catalogue!

How large are the classes? Do students receive enough individual attention from the professor?

Where do people study here? Where can I study early in the morning? Late in the evening?

How easy is it to work and go to school at the same time here? To pay rent in this area? Where do students with jobs like to work the best? What is work-study, and how easy is it to obtain that kind of job?

How well connected are the professors? A good professor will have spent years in the working world, and may often provide a liaison between you and an important internship, or even your first job. Will yours help you succeed beyond the classroom?

How easy/affordable is it to get tutoring for a class if I'm having a hard time? How popular are study groups at this school?

Finally, if you are a student that needs an organization to "get started," look into the many clubs and organizations that are unique to your campus in addition to sororities and fraternities. At some universities such as Southern Methodist University, Greek life is a "must" and can lead to a well-rounded social life of friends and activities. At other universities, such as Texas Woman's University, joining a community service or professional group is a viable option for making friends. At Harvard University, there are no sororities or fraternities. The concentration is on academics.

14. Housing options (dorms, apartments, living at home)

At home, perhaps your bedroom is a typical ten-foot-by-ten-foot room that you call your own. At college, your dorm room may be eight feet by eight feet and have a twin bed on each side of the room with a closet that might hold your winter coat. Housing should not be your number one priority but it does matter and in most cases, timing is everything, meaning, first come, first served for the best dorms. Most colleges require that freshmen live on campus the first year unless their home is in the same city. To learn more about housing options, e-mail or write the college and ask the following questions:

HOW TO SAY IT

What kind of student housing is available?

What is the policy on housing arrangements and requests by students for changes?

Are student housing facilities secure?

What is the university policy about possession of illegal drugs or alcohol in campus housing?

What is the policy about weapons on campus housing?

How many security officers are assigned to each dorm?

What kinds of vacancy opportunities do students in housing have on holidays?

What is the policy for having overnight guests in campus housing?

15. Extracurricular activities (sports, volunteer organizations)

The Homecoming games, Midnight Madness, face paint and the pom-poms will all be a blur years from now as you look back at college, but the school spirit that went along with those times will never be forgotten. It doesn't matter whether your school is number one in the Big Twelve or never wins a game, it's the roar of the crowd and the chants that will stick in your mind and you will carry with you for the rest of your life. So, don't pass this opportunity up—grab it, hold onto it and cherish it. This chance might not last for long, and when it's gone, you will long for it to return. Go to the Homecoming game, or any game for that matter. Promise yourself to see at least one football game and one basketball game per year—and go to other sport events like soccer, volleyball, and even tennis. It doesn't matter if the teams win or lose, it's all about the rush that you get while you are there with your fellow students cheering for your team and your school. It makes you feel proud and unified, all at the same time (The Daily Targum, *Rutgers University, 2000*).

Whether it's a great football team, hockey team, basketball team, or soccer team, donning your school jersey and getting out there with the rest of your fellow students is a feeling that most recall as one of the best times of their life. Once you graduate, you keep the memory with you and are able to bond with people in your professional life who recall the same feelings and excitement. Even if sports events are not completely your thing, do attend at least one or two games to understand the power of being part of a group of a hundred or thousand students on a cool autumn afternoon. It can be contagious. You will remember it forever.

If extracurricular activities are more up your alley, look into the multitude of organizations on college websites. At North Carolina State University, students can choose from the following list:

Academic Honors Groups

Organizations Related to
    Academic Majors

Service Organizations

Residence Hall Council

Intramural/Recreational Sports/
    Club Teams

Student Government

Student Judicial Board

Union Activities Board

Student Media

Visual/ Performing/Musical Arts
    Groups

Minority Student Groups

Religious/Political Issues Groups

HOW TO SAY IT

If you find yourself drawn to groups such as those in the previous list, write or e-mail the college like this:

Dear College of Interest,

I am thinking of applying to your institution and am interested in the types of extracurricular activities and groups that are available for membership on your campus. Would you kindly send me information on this topic? I would also be interested in hearing from any student representatives in groups for _____. My phone number is (901) 123-4567 and my e-mail is _____. I look forward to hearing from you soon.

Sincerely,
Susie Senior

Make Your Short List

Now that you have checked out the items that are the most important to you from your Miracle list, write down the names of six or seven colleges or universities that you are interested in, in their order of importance to you. Then either go to their websites, e-mail, or call them to see which of **your** top five items they have. Once you find out, list those on the right side of the page next to the college's name.

Now, Apply Yourself!

This chapter has hopefully given you some direction on how to choose the college or university that you should apply to. Now that you've gathered enough

Short List of Top College Choices

College/University: _____

Location: _____

Which of my top 5 items does this college have?
(List in any order.)

1._____

2._____

3._____

4._____

5._____

Other Notes:

_____

_____

_____

_____

_____

information on the top six colleges of your choice, apply to all of them. This is a time to begin trusting your instincts. If a place feels right, that's important. More than one high school student came back and told me about visiting a college and immediately feeling at home. Those students typically stayed at that university and graduated. Other students visited top colleges and did not get that comfortable

---

College Trivia Quiz #2

What college did NFLer Mike McKenzie attend?

a) Memphis
b) Cincinnati
c) Kentucky
d) Tennessee-Martin

---

feeling during an interview or tour. When a few opted to go because it was a top college, they often transferred to a more comfortable college that fit their needs. You are choosing a new home away from home for the next four years. This is one of many big decisions that you will make in your life. Start off by examining all of the factors in this chapter and making the logical choice that feels right to you.

On page 53 you will find a worksheet titled Short List of Top College Choices. Make six copies of this page and use them to organize your top six college choices.

Check Out the Required Tests and Documents

With your colleges chosen, the next few chapters will take you through the rigorous (remember that word?) process of taking the right aptitude tests, filling out the application itself, getting recommendations, and writing your essay. There is also a checklist included that you can use to keep track of everything that the colleges require you to do to get to the finish line. Keep your deadlines in a calendar on your dresser or in your cellular phone and refer to it often. Colleges are serious about their deadlines and requirements. Never fear, however; this book will make sure that you have all that you need to get stamped, sealed, and delivered to the college on time.

College Clues and Cues

On average, 20 to 25 percent of college-enrolled students are transfer students. Perhaps you are thinking of attending a community college instead of a four-year college, to get your basic courses out of the way. Or, you are set on attending a four-year college but wonder what you would do if that college didn't work out. What's important is to make sure that the courses you take will transfer later if you decide to move. Most college admissions staff members can answer questions about transferring to their college. In fact, with the right GPA, they are thrilled to talk to you about transferring. The following information is provided by Ithaca College in New York regarding their transfer policy. It's rather typical of most colleges:

High school graduates who have earned nine or more college credits or have enrolled full-time at another college are considered transfer students. You can apply anytime, but for most programs, your final year must be completed at Ithaca. Some programs, such as physical therapy, have different requirements. The Office of First Year Programs and Orientation offers a special Transfer Transition program for transfer students that provides academic advising, testing, and registration information.

ICTC provides a support network and social activities for all Ithaca College transfer students. You can normally get transfer credit for college-level courses taken at an accredited college or university, provided a grade of C- or better was earned. Each course is individually evaluated, and Ithaca reserves the right to disallow unacceptable courses (Ithaca.edu).

Things to consider if you are thinking of attending a community college first and plan to transfer later:

Check that your courses will transfer to the university before you take them. Many universities have a community college list of acceptable courses that they can give to you.

Choose a college major as soon as possible and check with your community college advisor on which courses would apply to your major.

Pay attention to admissions requirements and deadlines of the university for each semester.

Visit the schools that you are interested in transferring to.

Discuss your transfer plans with a counselor or advisor at the university.

College Clues and Cues
For Parents

One June evening around midnight, our youngest son, Ryan, a college junior at a state college, crept into our bedroom and whispered into my ear, "Mom, I think I want to transfer to Baylor." As a percussionist at the University of North Texas, a school famous for its music and percussion courses, we had thought that he was happy there.

We soon learned that while he loved the music department, the A-Line, and the marching band, he also loved film and telecommunications. He reminded us of the awards that he had gotten in high school for filmmaking. Then he said that he had just changed his mind on what he wanted to do. He had done some research and found that Baylor had a top telecommunications major. So after midnight, together, we got online and he applied to Baylor, luckily making the cutoff for transfer applications and having the GPA that Baylor required. He transferred that fall. His first year was terrific academically but miserable socially. Living in an off campus apartment (mostly because it was too late to get into a dorm), making friends was very difficult. The next year he lived on campus and things began to get dramatically better. We learned and he learned the perils and the rewards of transferring.

One reason this book goes into so many details about choosing the right college is because many students get to college and are then disappointed in their choice. If that happens to your student, consider the following conversations:

HOW TO SAY IT

"Tell me what you hope to achieve by transferring."

"What makes this college a better choice? Tell me what you have researched about it."

"Let's start by contacting the college you want to transfer to immediately, and find out the admissions policy, deadlines for admission, GPA requirements, and available housing."

"Since you are transferring, I am going to suggest (insist) that you find housing either on campus or as close as possible to campus for at least a semester to get yourself into the college atmosphere and feel comfortable."

"I would also like you to call a college advisor as soon as possible about what you will need to do to transfer courses from your current college to the new one. Make sure you have your current college catalogue handy so that course descriptions can be compared."

"If some of the credits don't transfer, you may not graduate as soon as you had hoped. So, we need to keep financial aid applications going."

The good news is that in the end, transferring to a different school may be the best decision your student will ever make. There are lots of hoops to jump through to transfer, and that helps students to recognize the importance of good decisions. But in the end, when your son or daughter does graduate, they will do so in the school they love with a major that fits who they are.

Oh, the Tests You Will Take

Written with Ryan Rose Weaver, BS,
Emerson University, 2006

Young cat, if you keep your eyes open enough, oh, the stuff you would learn! The most wonderful stuff!

—Dr. Seuss, Seuss-isms

When I worked as a high school counselor, I answered many questions from my students, especially sophomores and juniors, about the Preliminary Scholastic Aptitude Test/National Merit Scholarship Qualifying Test, or the PSAT/NM-SQT, which is administered yearly in October (registration takes place in early September). These "frequently asked questions" included:

Should I take the PSAT? Why?

How much does it cost?

Where do I take it?

Isn't the PSAT just a practice test?

Should I study for it?

What will the results mean?

How will it help me get into college?

Later in the fall, I saw the same students rush frantically into my office with questions about the SAT.

Should I study for the SAT?
What should I study for the SAT?
Do I need to take the ACT as well?
Do community colleges require the SAT or ACT?

Whether these students were interested in attending a top-tier school or simply fulfilling the requirements they needed to enter their local community college, they all had one thing in common: They had neglected to realize (or their counselors had neglected to tell them) that taking the PSAT, SAT, ACT, and the SAT Subject Tests, which for many was a nonnegotiable part of applying to college, would require extra planning on their part. After all, most students have taken hundreds of tests given by teachers by the time they enter their junior year, and haven't had much choice in the matter. But because all of the tests in the SAT family are administered either partially or wholly by an organization outside the school, known as the College Board—which also administers the Advanced Placement (AP) and College-Level Examination Program (CLEP)—students must make their own arrangements to take the test. It also takes planning because it requires students to register and to pay the College Board a fee for processing the test (low-income-level students are eligible for fee waivers), which must be done more than a month in advance or else there is a late fee.

Wait No Longer!

The sad news for some of these students was that for every minute that they delayed the college admission process (some of them were seniors before they realized that they had to take these tests), their pool of colleges shrank. But together, we often pulled the facts together, got online and registered for the tests (sometimes on that day), and they took them. Some did surprisingly well, and some had to retake the test again in the spring. Time was of the essence for many of them, and the pressure was tough. Because the College Board is the one who sends on the tests to colleges as soon as they are graded, these colleges probably noticed the students' lack of planning, a first strike against them. For some state colleges with *rolling admissions* (meaning that you can apply at any time of the year) the students were welcomed after taking their tests and many of them were able to get in to some lower-tiered schools. For students applying to the private colleges, the process was more challenging. Many had missed the deadlines and had to settle for their second and third choice of college.

There is a better way. The better way is to *plan*. And not only does planning help you to get into the college of your choice, it impresses the college admissions staff. When interviewing many state and private admissions staff members for this book, I learned that they take serious notice when the student calls or inquires *early*. To them, a student that is organized is more likely to be an organized college student and that leads to successful college graduates.

So let's begin planning.

Practice Makes Perfect: Plan to Take the PSAT

While most students have heard their fill about the importance of the Scholastic Aptitude Test (SAT), for years by the time they take it, many do not hear about the Preliminary SAT/National Merit Scholarship Qualifying Test (PSAT/NMSQT) until late in their high school careers—sometimes too late to make a difference. And the PSAT, believe it or not, can make a big difference in helping you succeed in your college entry process, and not just because it provides you with practice for the Big Test at the end of the year. Like the SAT, it can also help you gain financial aid for college.

While you may have heard that colleges will pay top dollar for those that score high on the SAT, there is an organization that will reward you with scholarship money for doing well on the PSAT. The PSAT is conducted as a joint program between the College Board and the National Merit Scholarship Corporation (NMSC). The NMSC uses these test scores to determine the recipients of their scholarship program, in which finalists can go on to earn $2,500 in money for college. Out of the 1.4 million students who take the test each year, another 50,000 will be recognized by the program and may be eligible for another range of scholarships provided by the companies and organizations associated with the NMSC. Because applying for scholarships to pay for college can often be as time-consuming as applying for college itself, and doing well on the SAT can garner you even more financial support from your school, studying and doing well on the PSAT can mean a big payoff for you. And considering the PSAT only costs $12, and can be free for low-income students who qualify for a fee waiver, it is an investment worth considering for every student, regardless of their financial situation or future plans.

As you might imagine, the Preliminary SAT is designed to be very similar to the SAT in structure, with reading/writing and math sections. Unlike the SAT, however, it is a third shorter (two hours and ten minutes versus three hours and forty-five minutes), is designed to be slightly easier than the SAT, and it does not currently have an essay-writing portion. Here's what to expect on the PSAT:

- 48 multiple-choice critical reading questions, which will require you to read an essay, or you will be asked to complete a sentence using multiple choice

- 39 multiple-choice writing skills questions, which test your knowledge of proper grammar and your ability to recognize grammatical errors

- 28 multiple-choice math questions and 10 grid math questions that cover concepts in algebra, geometry, data analysis, measurement, and statistics and probability

Why and How to Prepare for the PSAT and SAT

Many students wonder about the best way to study for the PSAT, and by extension the SAT. Many feel that it depends on "luck" or natural genius, and that they have little control over their scores. Nothing could be further from the truth. It may seem funny to practice to take a practice test to then take a real test, but if you get used to the way it looks and sounds, you will likely be less stressed, intimidated, and confused when you finally see the final version. You wouldn't show up to a band concert without looking at the sheet music, or step onstage at a recital without first knowing the choreography, or expect to run a winning touchdown without looking at the playbook. Moreover, you couldn't do these things well if you hadn't done scales for weeks, stood on toe for months, or run laps every day to build up your skills. Practicing your testing skills, just like practicing the movements of your fingers on an instrument or the movements of your feet in a dance or a sports play, will make the difference in your "scoring big" on the test.

Another common misconception students have is that they should be enrolled in a special program for practicing the test, or they will miss out. It is true that there are many different preparation courses and study guides for College Board tests that promise to prepare you or even to improve your scores, but regardless of what you or your parents can afford to do to help you get ready, just remember: Every student, whether he or she is rich or poor, organized or disorganized, in Honors English or remedial reading, or in AP calculus or basic algebra class, has the same amount of time to study before the test, and will have the same amount of time to answer the same forty-eight reading questions, thirty-nine writing questions, and twenty-eight math questions. The best way to prepare to answer them, therefore, is to practice answering them and see how you do.

You will also find that you actually save time on the test if you practice because the College Board often asks similar questions in the same format; their website's preparation is even based on this concept, and discusses how to answer each question "type." If you are used to seeing questions that contain the same sentence elements, you will understand each one more quickly—and you can spend more time pondering the answers.

Remember These Resources!

There are many free resources that will help you practice for the PSAT and the SAT throughout the year. Your first stop should be the College Board website, at www.collegeboard.com, which has many online resources, including a calendar to help you manage your time year by year, and sections full of practice questions and tests. It even includes a free sign-up service that e-mails you one practice question a day. This may be an appealing option to students who spend a lot of time doing work (or playing) on their computers, or for those who prefer to study a little bit at a time rather than "cramming." Think of it as a much less invasive version of your teachers and parents, reminding you: "Did you spend some time studying for the PSAT today?"

Another free resource is www.studyguidezone.com, a website designed by educators concerned about universal access to testing resources for all students. This site contains a directory for several different tests and a comprehensive Study Resources section that goes beyond the test, offering plain-English insights into keeping yourself motivated during class, facing your math fears or test stress, and even giving you reasons to be excited for college—an emotion that is often lost during the frightening, stressful college application process.

The website www.sparknotes.com is most commonly known for providing synopses of books for English students, but it also contains a set of helpful tips on the SAT essay at www.sparknotes.com/testprep/books/newsat/powertactics/essay/. Read here about "Essential Strategies" for managing your time and organizing your essay, as well as "15 Most Common Mistakes" (yikes!) such as focusing on the length rather than the content of your essay or forgetting to actually take a position on the prompt.

Finally, www.number2.com provides preparation for both the SAT and the ACT tests, so if you are planning to take both, this site may represent a convenient one-stop shop for you and your parents as you peruse sample questions or try to decide which test you should take.

Use Your PSAT Score to Study for the SAT

Because the PSAT is designed to be the ultimate practice test for the SAT, you should make sure to study as much as you can beforehand so that you gain an accurate idea of your strengths and weaknesses. Many students have an area of specialty, and you might find that you did well on the verbal but "bomb" on the math section or vice versa. The busier you are, the more valuable this information can be, because you will know exactly how to spend your time: Why spend hours reading the dictionary if your verbal score was satisfactory? You should also note, however, that regardless of how you score on the PSAT, most students are expected to score higher on the SAT than on the PSAT, sometimes significantly higher. This is because during the year, you will gain more knowledge and reinforce the knowledge you already have, and you will likely practice the test over and over (and if you aren't planning to do this, you should begin now!), and like anything at which you practice hard, you will get better!

There are some key differences that you should note before moving on to the other areas of this chapter between the PSAT and the SAT, especially when it comes to deadlines and fees. There will be more information on the SAT in the following section, but make sure that you have planned and registered for both early in your junior year—or act on them as quickly as possible if you haven't! Check out the chapter on meeting deadlines and programming them into your calendar.

Similarities and Differences Between the PSAT and SAT

Similarities:

- Both are formal tests created by the College Board.

- Both require preregistration a month or more in advance.

- Both require students to pay a fee, unless they qualify to take it for free.

- Both contain similar wording and questions on the same subjects.

- Both are forwarded to the student's colleges of choice upon request by the College Board.

Differences:

- The PSAT is administered by high schools. The SAT is administered by the College Board.

- PSAT registration takes place at the high school and costs approximately $12.

- The PSAT is administered only once a year, in October. The SAT is administered seven times a year, from October to June.

- The PSAT is not required for college entrance, but is required for consideration in the National Merit Scholarship Program.

- The SAT and ACT are the standardized tests required by colleges, but do not make students eligible for any additional funding other than that decided by their colleges of choice.

- Students take the PSAT only once, in the fall of their junior year. The College Board recommends that students take the SAT during the winter of their junior year, but students may register between October and June, and may retake it until they are satisfied with their score (many do).

- The PSAT contains math and verbal multiple-choice portions. The SAT now contains an essay question in addition to these portions. Students must practice this portion on their own until they take the test.

Ask your counselor in the beginning of your junior year about registering for the PSAT. The date is determined by your school. SAT registration takes place online. Fees are approximately $42. You may ask counselors to help with the registration process and fee waivers, but you must register yourself online at www.collegeboard.com. Dates are determined by the College Board.

Take the SAT!

Register early. Get your *CEEB/ACT codes* from your school or registrar. Once you've gotten your registration and fees into the College Board (early, of course), you've received your scores from the PSAT (stunning, of course), and you've been practicing your SAT questions (daily, of course), you are on track to doing well on the SAT and you know from your PSAT scores that you have strengths and weaknesses in certain areas. If you are equally strong in verbal and math areas, you are very fortunate—but you should plan to study twice as hard to bring up your scores in both areas. You will also need to add essay writing to your repertoire of skills, because as of January 2005, the SAT now contains a long-form essay composition section in addition to its multiple-choice requirements. This brings the final potential score on the SAT from 1600 points split between the math and verbal portions to a total of 2400, with each having a total of 200 to 800 points possible. The way these are divided on the test (which takes three hours and forty-five minutes) is as follows:

- 25 minutes to complete the essay composition section, which will always come first

- Six 25-minute sections of verbal and math questions (sections can be in varying order to discourage cheating or bias)

- Two 20-minute sections (one critical reading, one math, in varying order)

- A 10-minute multiple-choice writing section, which will always be the final section.

HOW TO SAY IT

WRITING AN EXCEPTIONAL ESSAY

As a senior, you will write several essays for your college applications, so honing in on perfecting this skill will be valuable to you very soon in your high school career. When it comes to writing the SAT essay, there seem to be many suggestions and few shortcuts. Most of the scorers of the SAT essay will have seen everything before so they won't give a high score just because the essay is long or uses literary examples. They are looking for good writing, period. They also know that this is the "first draft." It won't be perfect, obviously, but should show preliminary thoughts and ideas that could evolve into a master essay. They want to see insight, a point of view with reasons that mean you gave the prompt (topic) a lot of thought, and the use of language in a skillful manner. In particular, the *components of good writing* will fall into these four categories:

1. Your position: Is it strong? Is it clear?

2. Your examples: Are they relevant to the topic? How well do you use them to develop your argument?

3. Your organization: Can you write an essay that flows from one idea to the other, even when writing by hand within a limited amount of time? Are each of your paragraphs well developed and do they have proper transitions? Do you spend an appropriate amount of time on each point? Does the essay overall seem a well-organized whole?

4. Your command of language: Does your sentence construction, grammar, and word choice show an ability to craft varied, sophisticated, and interesting prose?

Making the Grade: The SAT Rubric

According to the College Board, each essay reader will use the grading system below, assigning the composition a score of 1 to 6, as follows:

6—Outstanding, demonstrating clear and consistent mastery. A few minor errors will be permissible.

5—Effective, demonstrating reasonably consistent mastery. Occasional errors or lapses in quality will be permissible.

4—Competent, demonstrating adequate mastery. Lapses in quality expected.

3—Inadequate, but demonstrates developing mastery. Will be marked by one or more major weaknesses.

2—Seriously limited, demonstrating little mastery. Will be flawed by one or more major weaknesses.

1—Fundamentally lacking, demonstrating little or no mastery. Will be severely flawed by major weaknesses.

Now let's examine an actual SAT essay to see how this comes together. This prompt, essay and analysis were provided by www.sparknotes.com.

Prompt: "There's no success like failure."
What is your view on the idea that success can begin with failure? In an essay, support your position using an example (or examples) from literature, the arts, history, current events, politics, science and technology, or from your personal experience or observation.

As you read the following essays, pay attention to the grader's comments which appear in parentheses.

Learning the lessons taught by failure is a sure route to success. (THESIS STATEMENT) The United States of America can be seen as a success that emerged from failure: by learning from the weaknesses of the Articles of Confederation, the founding fathers were able to create the Constitution,

the document on which America is built. (BEST SUPPORTING EXAMPLE [1]) Google, Inc., the popular Internet search engine, is another example of a success that arose from learning from failure, though in this case Google learned from the failures of its competitors. (NEXT BEST SUPPORTING EXAMPLE [2]) Another example that shows how success can arise from failure is the story of Rod Johnson, who started a recruiting firm that arose from Johnson's personal experience of being laid off. (NEXT BEST SUPPORTING EXAMPLE [3])

The United States, the first great democracy of the modern world, is also one of the best examples of a success achieved by studying and learning from earlier failures. (TOPIC SENTENCE FOR EXAMPLE 1) After just five years of living under the Articles of Confederation, which established the United States of America as a single country for the first time, the states realized that they needed a new document and a new more powerful government. In 1786, the Annapolis convention was convened. The result, three years later, was the Constitution, which created a more powerful central government while also maintaining the integrity of the states. By learning from the failure of the Articles, the founding fathers created the founding document of a country that has become both the most powerful country in the world and a beacon of democracy. (FOUR DEVELOPMENT SENTENCES TO SUPPORT EXAMPLE 1)

Unlike the United States, which had its fair share of ups and downs over the years, the Internet search engine company Google, Inc., has suffered few setbacks since it went into business in the late 1990s. (TOPIC SENTENCE FOR EXAMPLE 2) Google has succeeded by studying the failures of other companies in order to help it innovate its technology and business model. Google identified and solved the problem of assessing the quality of search results by using the number of links pointing to a page as an indicator of the number of people who find the page valuable. Suddenly, Google's search results became far more accurate and reliable than those from other companies, and now Google's dominance in the field of Internet search is almost absolute. (THREE DEVELOPMENT SENTENCES TO SUPPORT EXAMPLE 2)

The example of Rod Johnson's success as an entrepreneur in the recruiting field also shows how effective learning from mistakes and failure can be. (TOPIC SENTENCE FOR EXAMPLE 3) Rather than accept his failure after being laid off, Johnson decided to study it. After a month of research, Johnson realized that his failure to find a new job resulted primarily from the inefficiency of the local job placement agencies, not from his own deficiencies. A month later, Johnson created Johnson Staffing to correct this weakness in the job placement sector. Today Johnson Staffing is the largest job placement agency in South Carolina, and is in the process of expanding into a national corporation. (FOUR DEVELOPMENT SENTENCES TO SUPPORT EXAMPLE 3)

Failure is often seen as embarrassing, something to be denied and hidden. But as the examples of the U.S. Constitution, Google, and Rod Johnson prove, if an individual, organization, or even a nation is strong enough to face and study its failure, then that failure can become a powerful teacher. (THESIS STATEMENT REPHRASED IN BROADER WAY THAT PUSHES IT FURTHER) The examples of history and business demonstrate that failure can be the best catalyst of success, but only if people have the courage to face it head on. (www.sparknotes.com)

The Grade: 6

The writer of this essay makes a statement early and stays with his opinion from the first sentence to the last one. He uses three examples from a variety of areas, from internet technology to history and politics. Then, he adds a profile of an entrepreneur and supports the thesis statement's position. The writer's use of language is solid and clear throughout the essay. He does not take risks to sound too intelligent, and instead, chooses out of the ordinary words such as *beacon*, *deficiencies*, and *innovate* to add a spark of creativity that conveys his personality.

Last, his grammar is appropriate and he varies the lengths of the sentences to add interest and get the reader's attention.

Writing the essay for the SAT will come during a time when you are stressed yet want to show off your language skills. As mentioned early in this chapter, practice writing essays and show them to your English teacher for editing and feedback. Go to www.collegeboard.com for a sample of topics to write about. Then, use the four components of good writing to hone your skills and ease your anxiety about the essay.

Fact: You May Need to Take the SAT II

Many students, in their rush to make sure they are signed up for the SAT I: Reasoning Test, do not have time to investigate the reasons why the SAT has a handful of other "Subject Tests." These tests delve more deeply into areas not covered in the SAT I. It is not as important to take a Subject Test as it might be to take another standardized test such as the ACT for college entrance purposes. However, a Subject Test might be required by your college of choice, and it is very important that you research this information at the same time that you are registering for your PSAT and SAT so that you can be sure to meet all of the requirements for your college of choice—or you might be disappointed to find that your very selective school will not accept your application because you have missed this commonly overlooked detail. Don't let that happen to you!

Your college may ask you to take an SAT II test for the following reasons:

1. The school is a highly selective school and requires all applicants to complete one SAT II as a way to further qualify their applicant pool. One example of this is Cornell University, which requires that all applicants to all of its colleges take the SAT II in Mathematics, with the exception of its College of Arts and Sciences, which requires that the applicant take any two SAT II Subject Tests.

2. The school may consider waiving certain freshman requirements if you demonstrate adequate aptitude in the subject on the corresponding SAT II Test.

That can be good news.

3. The school wishes to test your skills in a particular language, either to confirm that you meet their language prerequisite requirements or to allow you to waive that requirement and bypass language classes in college.

The SAT II Subject Tests include subjects you may have studied vigorously in high school and may plan to pursue as a field of study in college, but are not included on the SAT I, such as history, literature, and science. The full list is as follows:

English
Literature

History and Social Studies
U.S. History (formerly American History and Social Studies)
World History

Mathematics
Mathematics Level 1 (formerly Mathematics IC)
Mathematics Level 2 (formerly Mathematics IIC)

Science
Biology E/M
Chemistry
Physics

Languages

Chinese with Listening	Spanish with Listening
French	Modern Hebrew
French with Listening	Italian
German	Latin
German with Listening	Japanese with Listening
Spanish	Korean with Listening

HOW TO SAY IT ON THE SAT II

According to the College Board, there are some helpful ways to approach taking the SAT II tests:

- Take a subject test when the course content is still fresh in your mind, such as at the end of the course.

- Learn how the test is organized. Check out www.collegeboard.com for examples of questions and test directions.

- Do the easy questions first. They are usually at the beginning of the group of questions and can stack up some points.

- Learn how the test is scored to lessen anxiety and formulate a strategy. You get one point for each right answer and you lose a fraction of a point for each wrong answer. If you omit a question, you neither lose or gain points.

- Steer away from guessing unless you can eliminate some answers from a question which may enable you to have a better chance of guessing it correctly.

- Use your test book to scratch out answers that you know are wrong but don't forget to write the correct answer on the answer sheet . . . that's what gets turned in for scoring.

Act Now: Plan to Take the ACT

The ACT is another standardized test that can offer colleges a way of viewing your knowledge. It has many similarities with the SAT and is weighed similarly in your college application. Some top-tier colleges are beginning to require an additional test in conjunction with the SAT, which can be an SAT Subject Test or the ACT. Some students perform better on either the ACT or the SAT format so taking a test in a different format can provide you with an entirely different perspective on what you've learned. If you are planning to take the SAT multiple times in order to get the results you like, you may consider looking to the ACT as another opportunity to achieve that elusive high score. Most colleges accept the ACT in lieu of the SAT; it has a similar testing rubric, with math and verbal sections (it also includes a science section). The ACT also added an essay writing component in early 2005, which remains optional for ACT takers. The fee ($43) is similar. The ACT is a widely available test and is the primary test for students in some states; according to the ACT official website (www.act.org), 1.2 million students took the ACT in 2006, with the highest numbers of students concentrated in Illinois, Ohio, Texas, Michigan, and Florida.

The ACT grading system differs from the SAT in some major ways, however. Instead of 2400 points, there are 36 total points available on the ACT, and the score received is an average of the four sections on the test: English, math, reading, and science, with an optional writing section that can change the average of the English and reading score. The breakdown of the sections is as follows:

English: 45 minutes, 75 questions
Math: 60 minutes, 60 questions
Reading: 35 minutes, 40 questions
Science: 35 minutes, 40 questions

The ACT Writing Test adds thirty minutes to the testing time.

Like the SAT, the ACT Writing Test is graded with a 1 to 6 rubric. If you take the ACT, your essay will be graded by two trained readers who decide on a rating of 1 through 6. If the two cannot agree on a score, a third reader settles the issue and gives a score. The readers also give constructive feedback on the essay. To receive a top score of 6, the following criteria has to be met:

According to www.act.org, essays that get the top score of 6 show a definite skill in responding to the prompt. The writer shows a clear understanding of the task by taking a position on the issue and developing a context that is critical. The writer examines many facets of the issue and names the complications and implications.

The writer elaborates on the subject and focuses on the specific issues of the prompt throughout the essay. The organization is clear. The sentences are sequenced properly, with the introduction and conclusion effective, clear, and developed in a manner that holds the reader's attention. There are little to no grammatical errors.

Let's examine a successful ACT writing sample. Here's a prompt and an essay from www.act.org:

Prompt: Educators debate extending high school to five years because of increasing demands on students from employers and colleges to participate in extracurricular activities and community service in addition to having high grades. Some educators support extending high school to five years because they think students need more time to achieve all that is expected of them. Other educators do not support extending high school to five years because they think students would lose interest in school and attendance would drop in the fifth year. In your opinion, should high school be extended to five years?

In your essay, take a position on this question. You may write about either one of the two points of view given, or you may present a different point of view on this question. Use specific reasons and examples to support your position.

Here's an example of an essay that answered this topic:

The Senior Itch—the incurable chafing we all crave to scratch. The cure? Graduation. As we progress through our high school years growing with wisdom and maturity, we all yearn for freedom. Yet what we desire most is not always what is best for us. Although most won't want to admit it, extending our high school career to five years would make an important and beneficial impact on our future. With the four years that are currently provided, there is not enough time for motivated students to accomplish their goals before college. Merely being accepted by a selective college or university requires much preplanned effort that is literally unavailable to students already concerned with grades and other activities.

Colleges look most thoroughly at how an applicant used his or her four years of high school. Leadership roles, a dedication to an organization, and a well-rounded, involved student is appealing to the most elite educational institutions. Often, students desire leadership positions in numerous extracurricular organizations, but face limiting regulations on the number of offices they may hold at one time. Even if a school doesn't limit students' involvement, students eventually reach the limits of what a twenty-four-hour day can hold. Too often, students cannot participate as much as they want in as many extracurricular activities as they want because there just isn't time. With an extra year of high school, those involved in more than one activity could successfully find the time to contribute to and to lead each one. Colleges would see a longer, more developed individual's résumé that included a time for each of their interests. The organizations would benefit from stronger student participation and the students would be recognized for their true efforts as well.

Because they struggle to gain leadership roles and become the well-rounded students colleges desire, the task of maintaining a respectable grade point average during high school is a struggle for many students. It is difficult to be involved in activities of interest while still keeping high grades. However, colleges don't consider this when they seek applicants with high grade point averages in their admissions pool. Elongating the span of high school would allow more students with both grades and activities on their agenda to spend more time focusing on each separate interest. Rather than feeling forced to crunch a large block of "weighted" classes together in hopes of elevating their GPA, students would find more time to spread out their difficult classes and make the most of every single year. With less pressure and more time, grades would improve for all dedicated students, as would the enjoyment of studying those subjects and the increased retention of what we learned in those classes.

Education aside, many high school students find that four years is not enough time to accomplish their varied goals. For instance, a student may desire a job in addition to school. The money they earn may help pay their way through college. With such a short preparation period before college, they can hardly be expected to make a successful life for themselves without the proper funds. Also, many students are interested in community service prior to attending college, but find they do not have enough time in the four-year high school period. Colleges are drawn to students with a rich assortment of community service and evidence of responsibilities such as holding a job, but students have a hard time finding the hours to put into these tasks.

High school is the foundation of the rest of our life. Like money in the bank, the investment of an additional year when we are young can make all the difference. With the additional time, motivated students would be able to become more involved in their schools, boost their grades, and find the time for a job and community service. Colleges admire these attributes, and for the sake of high school students' acceptance into these institutions, more time should be provided for their endeavors. High school students work hard toward their future. Another year would help ensure their success.

Here are some responses from the graders of this essay, which earned a 6.

This essay demonstrates effective skill in responding to the writing task. The essay takes a position on the issue (extending our high school career to five years would make an important and beneficial impact on our future) *and offers a critical context for discussion* (Yet what we desire most is not always what is best for us). *Complexity is addressed as the writer anticipates and responds to a counterargument to the discussion* (Even if a school doesn't limit students' involvement, students eventually reach the limits of what a twenty-four-hour day can hold). *Development is ample, specific, and logical, discussing most ideas fully in terms of the resulting implications* (Colleges would see a longer, more developed individual's résumé that included a time for each of their interests. The organizations would benefit from stronger student participation and the students would be recognized for their true efforts as well). *Clear focus on the specific issue in the prompt is maintained.*

Organization of the essay is clear though predictable. Most of the essay demonstrates logical sequencing of ideas (It is difficult to be involved in activities of interest while still keeping high grades. However, colleges don't consider this when they seek applicants with high grade point averages in their admissions pool. Elongating the span of high school would allow more students with both grades and activities on their agenda to spend more time focusing on each separate interest). *Transitions are used throughout the essay* (although, even if, however, rather than) *and are often integrated into the essay* (Because they struggle to gain leadership roles and become the well-rounded students colleges desire, the task of maintaining a respectable grade point average during high school is a struggle for many students). *The conclusion and especially the introduction are effective and well developed. (www.act.org)*

HOW TO SAY IT

TIPS FOR *BOTH* THE ACT AND SAT ESSAYS

1. *Pay close attention to the prompt*. The prompt is meant to provoke your thinking on a topic. Let your opinions go wild for a moment and then

come up with an opening sentence that is strong and characteristic of your opinion on the subject. The first sentence should set the tone of the essay and should then be followed by sentences that support the opinion expressed in that first sentence.

2. *Develop your thinking—with time in mind.* Take time to develop your thoughts and explain them thoroughly. You may have big plans for your essay, but you may wish to outline them first, allotting a certain amount of time for each paragraph. You may be a wonderful and stylish writer with a flair for argument, but if you get bogged down explaining your first point and never reach your brilliant conclusion, it will be hard to show your readers the proof of this potential. Use scratch paper to develop a list of your thoughts. Pick the most convincing ones and cross out the others. As you develop your supportive sentences, ask yourself these questions:

> What are the main ideas that I am trying to convey to the reader?

> What sentences can I write to convey the point? How can I write them so that I will make the point stronger and more concise?

> Are the details in the sentences essential to the point?

> Am I using correct grammar?

3. *Speak your mind.* You are writing about your own opinion, so express it and use "I." Give examples from your own knowledge, life, personal experiences, and activities to support your opinion. Use language that is unique and creative. This is your time to impress the reader that you are college material because you desire to learn, process, and contribute to your world. Sell yourself by dipping into your own resources and proving that you know what you are talking about. For example, if a prompt was "The power of humor," think of saying something like:

> *"Without humor, one can't know when life should or should not be taken seriously. How can we survive the disappointments that*

life brings each of us without humor? I remember a day when I struck out at the softball finals, broke up with my boyfriend, and came home to find that my dog had eaten my term paper. I cried, he licked my face, and then we both rolled around on the ground, while I laughed hysterically. Humor was all I needed to realize that I would get through the day."

Just Keep Studying, Just Keep Studying

The national average SAT score is 1518. The average ACT score is 20.9. Don't fret if your first test results aren't as high as you had hoped for. Retaking the test today is a common activity. Each time you receive a score, determine your weakest areas and bone up by studying one of the test prep booklets in your library or bookstore.

Start studying for the tests beginning at least three months in advance. Look over practice tests at websites such as www.number2.com, which will send you a set of practice questions every day, automatically, and practice the test so that you become familiar with the format. Then the night before, get lots of rest, and don't study. You will either know it by then or not. On the day of the test, drink lots of water . . . it's been shown to improve concentration by 70 percent. Eat breakfast; take a sweater and lots of sharpened pencils with you. These things really make a difference.

Finally, lessen your anxiety on test day by knowing that the test you will take is only one of the factors that will get you into college. The next chapter on applications will explain that more. On the way to the test, remember the things you have already accomplished in your life and how you accomplished them. High school graduation is on the horizon. You will soon become an adult. You've made a decision to go to college. These are milestones. The test is just one more.

College Trivia Quiz #3

What does John Lithgow, the actor who appeared on *3rd Rock from the Sun,* have in common with John Adams, John Quincy Adams, and John Kennedy?

College Clues and Cues

If you have a high GPA but your SAT score is below average, you should still apply to a top school. Your high school GPA gets the primary consideration, then your academic rigor (how many AP, IB, Honors classes you took), your test scores, your involvement in extracurricular activities, your employment, and your interests and dreams. Altogether these factors make up a neat package that the admissions staff considers.

So if you are a junior, sign up for a few more honors courses and take a chance on an AP or IB course. Volunteer in your community. Get a job that you feel proud of and stick with it for at least six months to show loyalty and consistency. Take a dual-credit college course. If you are a senior, study hard and participate in your classes with all your might so that your grades and recommendation letters stand out among the rest. Take dual college courses and sign up to participate in the fall of your senior year in as many activities as possible. The more you stay active in your last high school years, the more fun you will have and the better prepared you will be for the next four years. The admissions staff will notice.

College Clues and Cues
For Parents

Your son or daughter may be chanting to you what Bob Dylan sang to us, "The times, they are a-changin'," and they are right. The SAT and ACT that you and I took has changed. The format is different and the questions are tougher. Students are encouraged to take preparatory courses and study regularly for the big day. They compete with everyone at the same time. The pressure is tough. They want to please the college, themselves, and you.

There are the other factors to consider, too. Remember when your summer job could be just about anything from babysitting the neighbor's kids to washing cars or mowing lawns? You could even sit out a summer job and work for your parent's friends. Not now. If your kids mow yards today, they need to keep score of how many lawns and call it an individual business. If they babysit, they should also do so at the church, the shelter, or at a school event in addition to their neighbor's house. Today's college-bound juniors and seniors need real jobs and notable activities to compete and to prove that they are college material . . . and that's before they get into the college door.

And then there is the juggle of all those high school courses, SAT and ACT prep courses, extracurricular activities, community service, charity events, sports and cheerleading events, and even select sports and club cheerleading events. Add all of that up, include some sort of social life, family life, and stir well. These are the makings of a college-bound student. It can be overwhelming for your son or daughter. They may be taller than you but they are still your kids and they need your nurturing and encouragement now more than ever.

They also need your help balancing everything with applying to college on time. Offer to help them with deadlines and learn with them about the requirements that colleges have. Help your son or daughter by sitting down with them at a scheduled time and filling out items together. The following year, your house will have one less occupant. It will be quiet, so enjoy the time you can. Once they leave home for their freshman year, things change for you and for them and a whole new world opens up. Be a part of it now and you will remain a part later.

Apply, You Will.
Meet Deadlines, You Must!

Luke: "I don't believe it."
Yoda: "That is why you fail."
—The Empire Strikes Back

As a high school junior or high school senior, you are, by now, becoming aware of deadlines. They seem to be everywhere in your daily life. If you are a junior, you are learning about the importance of the PSAT, and maybe applying for drum major or the varsity team. If you are a senior, you are hearing about college admission deadlines, awards and sports banquets, as well as ACT and SAT tests. It's a lot to think about. Your school counselor should be able to help you find out the following facts that you will need to know before applying to college. If you don't have a school counselor, or can't get in to talk to her or him often, you can go online to the College Board site where you will find out everything you need to know about tests, test dates, and score reports. You can even e-mail someone at the College Board for information. Find out the following as soon as possible:

Test dates for the PSAT, ACT, and SAT.

Where you can obtain a practice test pamphlet—the College Board often provides schools with these. Write down a schedule to study for the PSAT, SAT, or ACT on the calendar.

How to sign up for SAT or ACT preparatory classes—ask the school counselor to suggest an additional study guide for the tests and to tell you of any programs or courses at local universities or even in your high school that you can take to prepare for the SAT or ACT tests.

Check out when the deadlines are for applications for local or national scholarships that will fit with your major and the college that you want to attend.

Learn how to log on to the *FAFSA* website. Ask your parent(s) when they will receive their W-2 forms from their employer in January. Find out when you will get one from your employer if you have a job. Keep the forms in a safe place. You have to have them for the FAFSA.

Use the Checklist!

On the next few pages is a checklist that you can program into your cell phone, computer, or paper calendar. The checklist contains a timeline of *very* important events and deadlines beginning in your junior year of high school and continuing through to graduation. If you put the information into your cell phone, set your alarm to go off to warn you to pay attention to a deadline. If you are more of a visual kind of person, buy a calendar and hang it up in a strategic place in your home or carry it in your school binder.

College Trivia Quiz #4

Which of the following universities does not have sororities and fraternities?

a) Boston University
b) Harvard University
c) Baylor University
d) University of Oregon

College Application Calendar of Events

Find out and put the following info on your calendar now. *Check each item off as you put it on your calendar.*

Junior Year of High School

SEPTEMBER

_____ PSAT registration deadline: _____

_____ PSAT test: _____

_____ SAT II registration for: Writing, Math 1, and one other choice.

_____ SAT II test dates: _____

_____ SAT registration deadline for the spring: _____

_____ SAT test date: _____

_____ Set a date this month to start your Experience Worksheet.

If you begin compiling it now, it will grow during your junior and senior year to an impressive one that you will use for letters of recommendation and on the Common Application. Save it on your computer and back it up on a CD or flash drive for safekeeping.

OCTOBER

_____ Sign up for extracurricular activities that are important for college applications.

_____ Take the PSAT test.

_____ Organize your tests and projects that come due this month in your classes. Write them down on your calendar. Your junior year grades are scrutinized closely by colleges, so study hard.

NOVEMBER

_____ Talk to your school counselor and find out when the PSAT results will be in. Note the date on the calendar and pick a date to check in with the counselor.

_____ SAT II test date.

_____ Fill in the Experience Worksheet this month with your activities and highlights for this school year

_____ Write down deadlines for projects and exams in school.

DECEMBER

_____ Take the December SAT II.

_____ Discuss the PSAT test results with your school counselor to learn what your score means. Ask about additional study guides for the SAT.

JANUARY

_____ Pick dates to start studying for the SAT and put them on your calendar.

_____ Find out the registration deadline for the March SAT test.

_____ Write down the test date on the calendar for March.

_____ Locate at least six colleges that you are interested in applying to. Look at websites, handbooks, videos, and talk to your school counselor and friends about which colleges you are interested in.

_____ Write down any new deadlines for activities during the spring semester.

FEBRUARY

_____ The spring semester of your junior year is the last semester that counts in your GPA/*class rank*. Study hard and get tutoring if necessary.

_____ Continue studying for the SAT. Write down study days.

_____ Write down project deadlines, examinations, and colleges you want to learn about this month. Find out which ones require the SAT II, and in the appendix begin filling out a College Fact Sheet on each college (see appendix).

MARCH

_____ Write down the registration deadline for the ACT.

_____ Write down the test date for the ACT.

_____ Write down the SAT registration deadlines.

_____ Write down the SAT test date.

_____ Write down the registration dates for AP exams.

_____ Write down the registration deadline for the SAT II.

_____ Write down the test dates for the SAT II tests for different subjects if you did not take it this month.

_____ Schedule college visits.

APRIL

_____ Keep visiting colleges and requesting brochures. See chapter 8 for questions to ask when you are on campus.

MAY

_____ Take the SAT.

_____ Take the SAT IIs.

_____ Take AP exams.

_____ Look for a summer job that demonstrates consistency and responsibility.

_____ Volunteer—work a few hours a week at a shelter or animal shelter a few hours per week. Help out a Boy Scout or Girl Scout troop. Donate time to a youth group at church. Write each activity down in *detail* on the Experience Worksheet in this chapter.

_____ Start requesting college applications and write down who you request them from on the College Fact Sheet in the appendix.

_____ Study for SAT II tests in June.

College Application Calendar of Events

Find out and put the following info on your calendar now. *Check each item off as you put it on your calendar.*

Senior Year of High School

SEPTEMBER

_____ Write down the registration deadlines for the SAT or ACT.

_____ Write down the SAT and ACT test dates.

_____ Write down deadlines for signing up for extracurricular activities.

_____ Start or update activities in your Experience Worksheet in this chapter. You need it for the Common Application and for your recommendation letters. Save it on your PC or your flash drive so that you can add to it throughout the year.

_____ Start listing the names of teachers that you have good relationships with and any other adults that you worked for or worked with for recommendation letters.

_____ Choose a day to ask for recommendation letters to be written. Take the supplies suggested in chapter 6 with you.

_____ Choose and write down a date to start working on your personal essay this month.

OCTOBER

_____ Take the SAT or ACT test.

_____ Research and enter all of the college application deadlines into your calendar. Note which ones accept the Common Application.

_____ Enter all of the information that you received on the College Fact Sheet in the appendix.

_____ Complete the Common Application this month and submit it by November 1.

_____ If you are interested in *Early Action* or *Early Decision,* check the deadline for mailing in applications.

_____ Check with the people who are writing letters of recommendation for you and remind them if necessary, of the deadline.

_____ Complete your college essay. Have an English teacher look it over and edit it for grammar.

_____ Request that your transcript be mailed to the colleges that you are applying to.

NOVEMBER

_____ Take the SAT IIs that are required by the colleges you are applying to.

_____ For colleges with rolling admissions decide on a date to submit your application.

_____ Choose a day this month to call or e-mail colleges about financial aid opportunities. Learn when the application deadlines are for financial aid. Write those dates down on your calendar. Besides the actual application deadlines, this one ranks second in importance. Don't forget.

_____ Make sure that all applications are submitted by Thanksgiving.

DECEMBER

_____ Take the SAT, SAT II, and ACT by this month. If you did not register, find out from your school counselor how you can do walk-in registration.

_____ If you are accepted by Early Decision, set a date to withdraw the applications to the other colleges by mail. (See more on Early Decision and Early Action in this chapter.)

_____ Choose a day in late December to begin filling out the FAFSA (Free Application for Federal Student Aid) online and save it online for e-mailing or mailing no later than February 1. You will need your parents' tax return and/or their W-2s as well as your own to finish the FAFSA.

JANUARY

_____ If you get the information from your parents and your own employer early, send in the FAFSA. Even if you can't get all of the information by February 1, still complete and mail or e-mail the FAFSA by that date, as the earlier you submit, the better. Even if your parents aren't going to pay for college, send in the FAFSA. You are in competition with everyone else so the early bird really does get the worm and the money in this case.

_____ Start inquiring about any scholarships that your community or school counselor might be aware of. Find out the deadlines and write down the dates on the calendar.

_____ Keep your nose in the books because if your grades slip too much, the college can "take back" their admissions offer. Really.

FEBRUARY

_____ E-mail or write to the colleges that you applied to and make sure that they received all of your materials such as test results, recommendation letters, the Common Application or their application. Do this early in the month so you have time to get items to them.

_____ Submit the FAFSA by February 1. Submit it online even if you don't have all of the information. Do not wait.

_____ This is a slow month, so study and spend time with friends and family.

MARCH

_____ When you are accepted by a college or university, mark your calendar for the last date the college will accept your acceptance form and the deposit.

_____ Write down the deadline for returning housing forms. Do it immediately for the best room, best dorm, and best roommate choices.

_____ Register for AP exams.

_____ Enjoy spring break with your high school friends and family.

APRIL

_____ Choose the college that you want to attend.

_____ Send in the deposit to the college that you decide to attend.

_____ Review the financial aid packages offered to you and accept or reject. Note the date that you need to respond, either in writing or online. If you forget, it goes away—so don't forget!

_____ If you are placed on a wait list, write the college and thank them for the opportunity. Write down the last date that they can notify you about admission so that you can accept another admission. Send them any additional letters of recommendation that you can obtain to help your chances.

_____ Find out dates for baccalaureate and graduation and put them on the calendar.

MAY

_____ Prepare for AP exams and finish your high school course work to the best of your ability. Most colleges will require a final transcript so do your best.

_____ Make your final college selection if you have not done so by now.

_____ Fill out all housing forms as soon as possible.

_____ If you have not heard from the financial aid department of the colleges that accepted you, call them. There may be an item that they need from you before giving you an award package. Sometimes, missing an item on the FAFSA slows things down.

_____ Write to the colleges that you have declined or send in your decline form. Thank them for their acceptance. You never know . . . you may end up transferring there.

JUNE

_____ Graduate.

_____ Order your final high school transcript to be sent to the college that you chose to attend.

_____ Make sure that you accepted/mailed the financial aid offers.

_____ Make sure that the housing request form was received and is being processed.

_____ Celebrate! You are about to experience the best year of your life.

College Clues and Cues

Here's a question to think about: With all of the extracurricular activities, AP classes, after-school commitments, and summer jobs, how *have* you done it all? Did you write down the dates that your tasks and required papers, applications for drill team, soccer, or baseball were due? Did your parents help you remember? Did you use your cell phone calendar or PC to help you remember with pop-up reminders? How did you do it all? You must have done something, or you wouldn't be graduating.

Going to college is just another step in the big scheme of things but it requires a bit more. In college your teachers might not be as forgiving as your high school teachers if you forget your lab supplies or homework assignment. This is the big time and all of the skills that you already have will help you through it.

So as you go through the next week, watch yourself with a new lens. Watch how you manage to keep your grades up with all of the activities you participate in. Watch how you do a mental checklist at times to make sure you have all you need for the day. These habits will help you as you begin working on college applications. The deadlines that you will find out about soon are *real* and if you don't pay attention, you will not be off to college when you graduate. Don't let that happen to you. If you need your parents to remind you to sit down and complete the application, ask them to do it. If you need to get a small whiteboard for your room to list all that you need to do, do it. If you need to learn how to program your cell phone to make an alarm sound when it's time to mail off your application, do it. This is great training . . . and it will get you to the college finish line.

College Clues and Cues
For Parents

Perhaps you are thinking, "I can't believe she's going to college next fall. She seems so young." Or, maybe you are thinking, "Will she ever get to those applications? How does she expect to make it in college without me constantly reminding her to get things done?" If you are asking any of those questions, count yourself among the other thousands of parents who think that they haven't a clue either. Then, realize that you do.

Begin by congratulating yourself on a job well done. She's almost there . . . graduation. What an accomplishment! It may seem like she needed you every step of the way (and she probably did) but a lot was done on her own. She motivated herself to get to early morning practices for drill team and late night "lock-ins" for student council fund-raisers. You were there in the shadows sometimes, and many times, in her room reminding her to do her homework. But in the end, she did them on her own.

But filling out applications is different. There are deadlines to meet and she has to meet them or she will still be at home next year. So help both you and your offspring identify *what gets them motivated and keeps them on task to complete important tasks.* To do so, consider the following questions:

> What kind of words or support do you and others use that motivate your future scholar to get things done on time?
>
> What kinds of rewards or consequences typically work to help your son or daughter get things done?
>
> Does it help if you or others sit down and help your son or daughter when a new assignment or project is due?

If your son or daughter were listening, what would they say would be the most helpful in regard to filling out college applications? What would they say you have done before that worked? What would they say others have done that worked?

Compile your answers and then go to your son or daughter and discuss what you have discovered. Then, do those that work. Typically, you may find that threats and yelling won't be at the top of their list. You might find, surprisingly, that sitting down with you on a slow-paced Sunday afternoon to fill out the application together might be at the top. Asking is the first step to cooperating and collaborating, two ways of communicating that will get you far during the college years.

This is a new transition. Use it as a way to reach and work with your son or daughter on this most important task. Don't give up. They are feeling the pressure of getting into college just as you might have felt it years ago. Their worries are bigger today since the competition is tougher and the requirements more rigorous. When you see little victories, cheer them on. When you see them feeling hopeless, remind them of the little victories. Together, make the process one to remember.

5

Mastering the Common Application

We are what we repeatedly do.
Excellence, then, is not an act but a habit.
—*Aristotle*

Quick, find a computer. Log on to the website of the first college on your short list of six colleges from chapter 2 and find out what application the college requires. If it is one of the 298 colleges in the United States that use the Common Application, you are in luck. Many of these colleges and universities use the form exclusively. Then go to https://app.commonapp.org.

Mark the common application website as a "favorite" on your computer. You will be coming back to it often. Now, let's learn about the different ways that you can apply to college.

Early Decision versus Early Action

Have you always been someone who could lay back and "go with the flow" or are you someone who would rather know what the cards say right now? Are you a planner? Do you like to commit to a project and then do what it takes to follow through? Do you trust your decisions or do you need a wealth of information to pick from before deciding on an option? Do you like to take your time on a project? Or, would you rather get it done so you don't have to worry?

Whatever your personality, preferences, or decision style, in addition to rolling applications and application deadlines, you may have another couple of terms to deal with: *early decision* and *early action.* They both sound rather final and rather definite, don't they? They are. They are two different kinds of opportunities offered by some colleges that will let you know where you will attend college by the end of December. That means while your friends wait out the *regular admission* option in the spring, you can sit back and enjoy the holidays if you choose either early decision or early action.

But which process is for you? They both inform you of your possible acceptance "early" but they each have a completely different outcome. Early action means simply that . . . a student is admitted early and can take action to solidify a position by sending in a deposit. In the early action process, a student can apply to several schools and learn in the fall of their senior year where he or she has the option of attending college the following fall. The main difference between early decision and early action is that in the early action process, the student has time to select the college from those that have admitted him early. The early decision option is stricter. This option means that the student, once accepted by a university, must withdraw all other applications from other schools.

The next two stories are examples of the kinds of students that utilize the early decision or early action opportunities in the most productive manner. As you read their stories, see if their circumstances match your goals.

Kent

Kent knew that he wanted to attend Texas A&M since he was five years old, when his father, a graduate, took him to his first game in College Station, Texas. A top graduate of an elite private school in Dallas, Kent dreamed of becoming an engineer just like his dad. Early decision was an easy decision for Kent. He knew that if he got into Texas A&M, he would have to withdraw every other application from other universities. He had always been committed to his decisions and now was no exception. So, he loaded up on every honors course and AP course offered, took a SAT preparatory course, and participated in some community service projects. He worked during the summer as an apprentice to an engineer and made sure he got recommendations from his boss and every teacher that gave him an A.

When he received his letter of acceptance from Texas A&M before Christmas, he knew he would receive his fair share of maroon sweatshirts during the holidays. He withdrew his applications from the other four schools that he had applied to for regular admission. Kent was fortunate in that Texas A&M gave him a full scholarship based on his GPA and outstanding test scores. He graduated last year at the top of his class.

Maria

Maria knew that she wanted to go away to college in the Northeast early in her sophomore year of high school. Having lived in rural New Mexico for most of her life, she was ready for a different culture and a different experience at college. She had attended a class taught by a teacher who had graduated from Boston College and the teacher had impressed Maria. She liked the teacher's open-mindedness toward Maria's writing. As a new writer on the school paper, Maria's articles were often chosen by Ms. Schmidt for their creativity and reader appeal. Like Kent, Maria took her share of AP courses in her junior and senior year and then studied on her own for both the SAT and ACT tests. (She couldn't afford the prep courses.) She applied to six schools in the Northeast, Boston College plus three Ivy League schools that were her preferred choices and two "safe" schools that she had researched as matching her profile.

Maria had worked during the summers, volunteered at a homeless shelter, and gotten recommendations from a few teachers that had attended schools in the northeast. She decided to go with the early action process so that if she were accepted, she could begin planning for a move across the country. The early decision did not fit Maria, since if accepted, she would have to attend without knowing the financial aid award, and that was a crucial part of her decision. When she got her acceptance letter from Boston College, she was elated. She looked over the financial aid package she received from Boston College in the spring and decided to wait a few weeks to see how the other colleges came through on their financial aid award packages. Then, along with her parents, Maria decided to accept the offer for admission from Boston College, which was the most generous offer that she received. However, the costs still meant that she would be taking out some student loans to supplement the grants the university offered her. Early action helped Maria to plan. She would keep her part-time job in the spring to save extra money for the move. She would also plan to register for two dual college credit classes at a local community college the summer prior to attending Boston College. That would save on tuition costs in the fall. She decided that getting dual credit would also help to keep her freshman year course load light and provide her with opportunities to explore Boston.

HOW TO SAY IT

Deciding whether to choose the early decision or early action totally depends on your planning. If you need the time to prepare for the move to another city, or to get a part-time job in the spring, either option will provide you with a direction earlier than regular admission. Other criteria that might help with these application options follows.

Say *yes* to early decision if:

- You know that you meet the college profile (GPA, test scores, recommendation letters, class rank).

- You have decided that a particular college is a perfect match for your academic goals.

- The college that you want to apply to is your first choice.

- You want to show how serious you are about attending a certain college.

Say *yes* to early action if:

- You need to know where you are going to attend the following year so that you can plan, work, and provide your family with enough time to get things in order for you.

- You want to know early in your senior year where you can attend college without feeling "bound" to attend. You can always decline.

- You want to show how serious you are about attending a certain college.

Say *no* to both early action and early decision if:

- You need the fall semester of your senior year to raise your GPA.

- You need to review the financial aid offers given to you in the spring before making a decision.

- You are unsure of which college to attend.

- You are a person that needs time to make a decision, or tends to change his mind.

- Your GPA and test scores are lower than the profile that the college usually accepts.

Note: Most of the applications that you submit for regular college admission are due in January at the latest. To be safe and competitive, you should complete them much earlier, closer to Thanksgiving.

Tips for the Filling in the Regular College Application

The Pen, in Black, Is Mighty

Somewhere in Grandma's basement or attic is a typewriter. Perhaps some of you know what they look like. If not, visit an antique store. Until about five years ago, using the typewriter on a college application wasn't unusual. Things have changed. If you are lucky enough to find one that works, and have received a paper application, use a typewriter and keep some correction fluid nearby for filling out the application. Or, you can just use a black pen and fill out the application. Print as legibly as possible, please! First impressions of how applications are completed are crucial!

If you are completing an online application, check out *when* the application is available online. That's right; the application may not be available at two in the morning. Check out the times and days that the application is available for downloading and completing and mark your calendar. On most applications you can complete parts of the application, save it for later, and then return to complete it. At this writing, most of the colleges interviewed preferred online applications and submissions. Many send notes back that the application has been received. If yours does not, do not hesitate to call the admissions office a few days after you submit your application to make sure that your application was received and not lost in cyberspace.

Picture Yourself

Your college may request a photograph of you. Control your urge to send in the one of you at the after prom party and instead, opt for your senior graduation photo, in wallet size. You don't necessarily have to send in the one of you in a cap and gown, just one that shows your smile and (almost) serious posture.

Supplemental and Regular Applications

If your college of choice does not utilize the Common Application, download its own application and fill it out online and submit. The college website will describe its preference for submitting the application or mailing it. If you decide to fill out a hard copy, download the application if available, print, fill it out, sign, and make a copy for yourself. Some applications will have a sheet for your high school to complete. After you mail in your application, deliver the high school request to the registrar at your high school, or to your school counselor. Make sure that if you are sending in your college application late in the fall semester, you request to have those grades included in the transcript. This may cause a slight delay but is important.

If you have taken college courses while in high school, make sure you request that your transcript is sent from this college. This is easily done by calling the college where you took courses and requesting to speak to the registrar. When you do call, have your Social Security number and address of the college ready to give to the clerk. There may be a very small fee to send the transcript. Some schools send them electronically, others by mail. Do this quickly after you mail in your application in case it takes more time.

Your college of choice may require a supplemental application. To find out, go to their website. Most colleges researched for this book that required supplemental applications asked for basically the same information as the Common Application.

Honors Programs

If you are interested in being accepted into an honors program at the university of your choice, make sure you take time to check every detail. While the GPA and test scores matter, the writing portion of the application is scrutinized more carefully for admission into honors programs. This is another situation where you want to brag about your achievements, extracurricular activities, volunteer activities, and club memberships. Make yourself an attractive applicant by writing about your dreams and aspirations and why this university is the coach that will take you there.

The Homeschooled Applicant: Stepping Out

If you have been homeschooled, the good news is that you can be as competitive as your regular-schooled counterparts. You will also have to do everything included in this chapter such as completing the Common Application, or the college's application, take the SAT or ACT, and gather recommendation letters. Many colleges will require you to take the SAT II Subjects Tests to gain a clear picture of your competency. For starters, make sure that your transcript is in order. For a terrific template to use as your high school transcript go to www.andrews.edu/homeschool/transcript.php.

Take note that some colleges researched require that the submission of a transcript should be from a homeschooling company that supplies a variety of curriculum products such as outlines and review books.

Since you did not attend a regular school where you would have received a SAT or ACT school code, go to the following website to obtain a homeschooling code: http://groups.yahoo.com/group/homeschool2college/.

At the same website, you and your parents will also be provided with valuable information on preparing for college during your last two years of high school. Keep up some extracurricular activities and fill out the Experience Worksheet in this chapter. These necessary activities will get you on track to competing with students from around the world and will help open the door to college.

Tavia Evans and Roxana Hadad, writers for FastWeb, an excellent resource for scholarships and grants, write:

As a homeschooled student, your trek to college has taken you off the beaten path. But even if you don't have the "typical" credentials colleges are looking for, you can still impress admissions counselors with a dazzling—and unique—application.

Successful homeschooled college applicants compile their courses and extracurricular activities into a sort of portfolio, explaining in detail what the courses entailed, including field trips, conversations with important people, etc. If you have produced artwork, photography, film, or music, submit samples of your work. Include essays, homework assignments that you are proud of, and a list of academic skills, competitions, and interests.

If you have volunteered during your high school years, or indulged in certain hobbies, explain them to the admissions staff. These activities show your passion and energy for your educational pursuits. If you can, get involved in your community and coach children's teams. Get the sponsoring agencies to write letters of recommendation for you. These will be more helpful than family members. If you are homeschooled, it is assumed that your family is supportive. You now need outside recommendations to add to your credibility.

Academically, take the AP tests and score as high as possible. Also take the College-Level Examination Program (CLEP) tests. If you can enroll in a college course at your local community college and do well, you will further your chances by indicating your ability to do well in a college course. As for the SAT and ACT tests, take the SAT II Subject Tests. The results can convey how well prepared you are in a variety of subjects. As a homeschooled student, these tests will carry more weight.

There may be more requirements for homeschooled students to submit to top colleges, but with the preparations described here, you will have a good chance of admission.

The Experiences of Your Lifetime, Please . . .

Your life is a story that you are about to tell to an admissions committee. How you tell it and how you say it will get the attention (or not) of those who write your letters of recommendation, review your application, and read your essays. This is not a time to be shy; brag about your traits and activities that have served you well up to now. It is a time to write about how you overcame afflictions, if any, or volunteered to help others. Whether or not you earned glorious awards in everything you did is not nearly as important as your involvement and commitment to activities that you felt good about. The importance of listing as many activities as possible on your application is obvious: They explain how involved and diverse you are and let the admissions staff know if you fit the school profile. Today, more colleges are asking for résumés as they convey quickly the assets of the applicant. In the chapter on recommendations, you will be given a template to compose a perfect résumé for your application, if the college requests it. For example, the following list of activities is listed on the United States Military Academy application. Observe the variety of activities and how they would translate into a candidate with leadership qualities:

Student Body Officer	Officer Non-School Club
Class President	Scouting
Officer School Club	Civil Air Patrol/ROTC
Member School Club	Eagle Scout/Gold Award
Editor School Publication	Senior Patrol Leader
School Band/Chorus	(https://secwww.admissions.
Boys/Girls State	usma.edu/forms/apply/cq.asp)
National Honor Society	

Use this list as an example of activities that you might have participated in but forgotten about. If you were a Boy or Girl Scout in elementary and junior high, mention it. It means you were part of a team and learned how to work with others. If you participated in Tae Kwon Do classes outside of school and became an officer or instructor, list that activity, since it conveys determination, consistency, and persistence. You are a variety of descriptions. Make sure that the admissions staff knows who you are, inside and outside of school.

On the next few pages is the Experience Worksheet, a type of self-interview that will ask you questions that the Common Application will ask and your references will need in order to write a killer recommendation. Filling out this worksheet will enable you to describe yourself in the most descriptive and flattering manner. And, to help you do so, the list on the next page will provide you with verbs that describe many different kinds of activities, studies, and situations. Notice that the words describe firm and confident actions. To add more interest, check out the additional list of adjectives that will make your descriptions of activities more vivid and colorful. You can refer to them when developing your essays and when completing your Experience Worksheet.

Once you complete the Experience Worksheet, read it over and ask yourself if it fully describes the person that you are. Have your parent(s) read it. Ask your school counselor to read it as well as one of your teachers. Then ask a friend to read it. Ask all of these "editors" if it describes a person rich in character, spirit, academics, community involvement, with a good work ethic and desire to succeed in spite of some challenges. If they all answer "yes, this is you," you are on your way. If the answer is "no" or "not quite" ask the "editor" what else you need to add. This is the first big step toward telling your story. Tell it well, with expression and excitement.

ACTION VERBS THAT SAY IT!

accomplished	completed	developed
achieved	computed	directed
answered	conducted	distributed
appeared	constructed	earned
applied	consulted	edited
arranged	contracted	entered
assisted	coordinated	established
awarded	counseled	evaluated
broadened	critiqued	experienced
brought	defined	explained
built	delegated	explored
changed	delivered	expressed
collected	demonstrated	filled
communicated	designed	focused
compiled	determined	formulated

garded	motivated	researched
guided	named	responded
helped	negotiated	selected
identified	operated	submitted
implemented	organized	succeeded
improved	participated	suggested
increased	performed	taught
initiated	persuaded	toured
installed	planned	trained
instructed	prepared	translated
introduced	presented	traveled
invented	published	tutored
involved	qualified	understood
joined	questioned	used
kept	raised	visited
learned	ranked	widened
led	received	won
made	recommended	worked
managed	reorganized	wrote
met	repaired	
monitored	represented	

ADJECTIVES THAT SAY IT!

amazing	happy	precious
beautiful	kind	pretty
better	magnificent	robust
big	many	round
bright	mighty	silly
friendly	new	spotty
funny	nice	tall
gigantic	nutritious	tame
great	ordinary	zany

Experience Worksheet

Name:_____

Phone #:_____

Student ID#:_____

Answer the following questions honestly and in complete sentences. Use action words from the Action Verbs That Say It list.

What is your GPA?_____

What is your Class Rank? _____ Is it weighted? _____ yes _____ no

Did you take AP (Advanced Placement) or IB (International Baccalaureate) classes? If so, list them here:

_____

_____

_____

_____

Were you on an honor roll or in an honors program? If so, list each year that you were actively involved:

_____

_____

_____

List all awards or honors in high school in order of importance with #1 being the highest award:

(Example: *I was selected to present my essay, "Leaders That Listen," at the Texas Association of Future High School Leaders where I won the top award and was given a plaque that now hangs in my school.*)

1._____
2._____
3._____
4._____
5._____

List all awards or honors outside of school, such as competitions on select sports, music, or cheerleading teams, church activities, or even employment activities, such as "employee of the month" in order of importance:

1._____
2._____
3._____
4._____
5._____

Were you elected into any leadership positions while in high school in student council, specific clubs, or sports activities or selected for programs such as peer helpers, tutors, or teacher's aids? If so, list them here in order of importance:

1._____
2._____
3._____

Did you take dual-credit college courses while in high school? If so, list the course names and when you took them:

_____

_____

_____

List your work history. Name the places that you have worked and how long you worked there. Include part-time as well as volunteer jobs. Start with the most recent job:

1._____
2._____
3._____
4._____
5._____

List all of your extracurricular activities for each year of high school (sports, clubs, teams, and other competitions or activities):

Freshman Year: _____
_____
_____

Sophomore Year: _____
_____
_____

Junior year: _____
_____
_____

Senior Year: _____
_____
_____

(Optional) What is your church affiliation? Did you participate in youth groups, mission trips, etc.? If so, list them along with the years that you participated:
_____
_____
_____
_____

Disciplinary actions: List any time when you were reprimanded for academic or behavioral issues that resulted in probation, suspension, or expulsion. Also add any explanation that you feel is important to stress to the admissions staff:

_____

_____

_____

_____

_____

Note: If you were never reprimanded during your school years, explain what characteristics and values helped you to maintain your good behavior:

_____

_____

Do you have a personal achievement that you are proud of (personal accomplishments in a work, hobby, or talent setting)? If so, write about it here:

_____

_____

_____

_____

_____

Have you had some challenges in your life (disadvantages due to being in a rural school with fewer rigorous courses, a certain socioeconomic status, parent's education/financial status, limited advising, physical, mental, or learning disabilities, illness, family situation, etc.)? Write about those challenges here:

_____

_____

_____

_____

_____

Explain how you were able to overcome these disadvantages and aspire to go to college:

_____
_____
_____
_____
_____

What are your particular or favorite interests? List them:
_____
_____
_____
_____
_____

What are your dreams for the future?
_____
_____
_____
_____
_____

If you surveyed teachers and friends at your school and asked them to list words that describe you, what words would they choose?

Teachers:_____
_____
Friends:_____
_____

Anatomy of the Common Application

The online Common Application allows you to move around from page to page, cut and paste text, and save multiple versions of your work. Once the application is complete, you can print it out, photocopy it, and send it off to any number of participating institutions. Many colleges now prefer that you submit your application by e-mail. As to the personal essay, which most colleges require, there are topics to choose from or the option of proposing a question of your own. Some colleges require additional information that is specific to that college's requirements and is downloadable at their website.

If the college that you want to apply to does accept the Common Application and does not expect other supplemental information, don't hesitate to send in an additional essay, artwork, or other work that you feel best explains who you are and what you have accomplished. They will be impressed that you took the time to send in your work to them to look over. It's called marketing yourself.

The Common Application obviously will save you time and effort, since you will be able to concentrate on writing one award-winning essay and filling out one application to send to several colleges for review. If a school gives the option of completing either the Common Application or their individual application, most colleges will sign a statement that the admissions staff will not give preference to either kind of application. Many of them will actually state this on their website formally. So, apply with confidence.

The Common Application consists of four separate forms:

1. the Application
2. the School Report
3. the Teacher Evaluation
4. the Midyear Report

In the next chapter on recommendations, you will find the rest of the Common Application, which includes teacher evaluations, midyear report, and final school report.

On the next few pages are the first four pages of the Common Application. Look it over, see how the items on your Experience Worksheet fit in, and start planning how you'll complete the real thing!

Other Applications to Juggle: Roommates and Financial Aid

So, what do housing applications for roommates and financial aid have in common? They both require you to be faster than lightning when it comes to submissions. The next two sections may seem less exciting than your acceptance letter but unless you read and follow through with the applications, you (a) may not be able to study due to loud music and stinky garbage and (b) may be sworn to three meals a day of ramen noodles.

When it comes to roommates, a lot of smaller colleges and universities really do try to match some of your own unique traits to those of other students, hoping to come up with a compatible situation for both of you. Some of you may have already chosen your roommate from your high school class. If that is so, your task of getting your housing application as soon as possible is even more crucial. But, if your preferred partner doesn't get assigned to your room, you might realize it could be a blessing in disguise.

Our oldest son, Roger, claims that his freshman roommate was someone he disliked the moment he laid eyes on him. Roger said that he spent most of his time tripping through clothes and computer cables that always seemed to be tangled up on the floor, pushing them under his roommate's bed, only to find that they migrated again to his side of the room later that day. But somehow the two of them made it through not only the first year but the second year, and today, seven years later, they are best friends, attending grad school together. Roger considers himself lucky to have met someone from another state and culture that he grew to like and respect.

My daughter's first three roommates all had families that owned jet airplanes. One of her roommate's mothers would whisk her daughter and her close friends away to New York City whenever the mood struck. I have to say

THE COMMON APPLICATION
For Undergraduate College Admission

2006-2007
FIRST-YEAR APPLICATION

The member colleges and universities fully support the use of this form. No distinction will be made between this form and a college's own. Please type or print in black ink. Be sure to follow the instructions on the cover page of the Common Application booklet to complete, copy, and submit your application to one or more of the member institutions.

OPTIONAL DECLARATION OF EARLY DECISION/EARLY ACTION/RESTRICTIVE EARLY ACTION

Complete this section **ONLY** if you are applying to one or more colleges under an early plan. It is your responsibility to follow that college's instructions regarding early admission, including obtaining and submitting any ED/EA/REA form provided by that college. **Do NOT complete this ED/EA/REA section on copies of your application submitted to colleges for Regular Decision or Rolling Admission.**

_____   ○ Early Decision ○ Early Action ○ Restrictive Early Action
College Name   *Deadline*

PERSONAL DATA

○ Male
○ Female

Legal name _____
*Enter name **exactly** as it appears on passports or other official documents. Last/Family   First   Middle (complete)   Jr., etc.*

Nickname (choose only one) _____   Former last name(s) if any _____

I am applying for the term beginning _____   Birth date _____
                                                                  mm/dd/yyyy

E-mail address _____

Permanent home address _____
                                       Number and Street   *Apartment #*

_____
              City or Town   *State/Province*   *Country*   *Zip/Postal*

Permanent home phone (_____) _____   Cell phone (_____) _____
                          Area Code   *Area Code*

If different from above, please give your mailing address for all admission correspondence.

Mailing address (from _____ to _____) _____
                    (mm/yyyy)   *(mm/yyyy)*   *Number and Street*   *Apartment #*

_____
              City or Town   *State/Province*   *Country*   *Zip/Postal*

If your mailing address is a boarding school, include name of school here: _____

Phone at mailing address (_____) _____   E-mail address _____
                            Area Code

Citizenship   ○ US citizen ○ Dual US citizen; please specify other country of citizenship _____

                 ○ US permanent resident visa; citizen of _____ Alien registration number _____

                 ○ Other citizenship _____
                                        Country(ies)   *Visa type*

                 If you are not a US citizen and live in the United States, how long have you been in the country? _____

Possible area(s) of academic concentration/major(s) _____   ○ Undecided

Possible career or professional plans _____   ○ Undecided

Will you be a candidate for financial aid? ○ Yes ○ No   If yes, the appropriate form(s) (e.g., FAFSA, CSS Profile) was/will be filed on _____.

The following items are optional. No information you provide will be used in a discriminatory manner.

Place of birth _____
                City   *State/Province*   *Country*

Social Security Number (if any) _____

First language, if other than English_____

Language spoken at home _____

Marital status: ○ Never married
                    ○ Married
                    ○ Widowed
                    ○ Separated
                    ○ Divorced (date _____)
                                        mm/dd/yyyy

If you wish to be identified with a particular ethnic group, please check all that apply:

○ African American, African, Black

○ Native American, Alaska Native (date enrolled _____
   Tribal affiliation _____)

○ Asian American (countries of family's origin _____)

○ Asian, incl. Indian Subcontinent (countries _____)

○ Hispanic, Latino (countries _____)

○ Mexican American, Chicano   ○ Native Hawaiian, Pacific Islander

○ Puerto Rican   ○ White or Caucasian

○ Other (specify _____)

© 2006 The Common Application, Inc.   AP-1/ **2006-2007**

EDUCATIONAL DATA

Secondary school you now attend (or from which you graduated) _____ Date of entry _____

Date of secondary graduation _____ Type of school ○ public ○ independent ○ parochial ○ home school

Address _____ CEEB/ACT Code _____

        Number and Street   *Apartment #*

_____

    City or Town   *State/Province*   *Country*   *Zip/Postal Code*

Counselor's name (Mr./Ms./Dr., etc.) _____ Counselor's e-mail _____

Title _____ Phone (____) _____ Fax (____) _____

         Area Code   *Number*   *Ext.*   *Area Code*   *Number*

List all other secondary schools, including summer schools as well as summer and other programs you have attended, beginning with ninth grade.

Name of School	Location (City, State/Province, Zip/Postal Code, Country)	Dates At
_____	_____	_____
_____	_____	_____
_____	_____	_____

List all colleges/universities at which you have taken courses for credit; list names of courses taken and grades earned on a separate sheet. Please have an official transcript sent from each institution as soon as possible.

Name of College/University & CEEB/ACT Code	Location (City, State/Province, Zip/Postal Code, Country)	Degree Candidate?	Dates Attended	Earned
_____	_____	○ Yes ○ No	_____	_____
_____	_____	○ Yes ○ No	_____	_____
_____	_____	○ Yes ○ No	_____	_____

If you received a GED, list date: _____ (Official scores must be sent from the testing agency.)

○ Not currently attending school. ○ Graduated from secondary school early.

If your education has been interrupted for any reason, please describe in detail on a separate sheet your activities since last enrolled.

TEST INFORMATION

Be sure to note the tests required for each institution to which you are applying. The official scores from the appropriate testing agency must be submitted to each institution as soon as possible. Please self-report your test scores below. *If you would **also** like to self-report your AP or IB scores, please list them in the Academic Honors section.*

ACT	Date taken/ to be taken	English	Math	Reading	Science	Composite	Combination English/ Writing
	Date taken/ to be taken	English	Math	Reading	Science	Composite	Combination English/ Writing
	Date taken/ to be taken	English	Math	Reading	Science	Composite	Combination English/ Writing

SAT I or SAT Reasoning Tests	Date taken/ to be taken	Verbal/ Critical Reading	Math	Writing	Date taken/ to be taken	Verbal/ Critical Reading	Math	Writing	Date taken/ to be taken	Verbal/ Critical Reading	Math	Writing

SAT II or Subject Tests	Date taken/ to be taken	Subject	Score	Date taken/ to be taken	Subject	Score	Date taken/ to be taken	Subject	Score
	Date taken/ to be taken	Subject	Score	Date taken/ to be taken	Subject	Score	Date taken/ to be taken	Subject	Score

Test of English as a second language (TOEFL or other exam)	Test	Date taken/ to be taken	Score	Test	Date taken/ to be taken	Score

FAMILY

Parent /Guardian 1 _____
          Last/Family   *First*   *Middle*   *Title*   *Gender*

○ Mother ○ Father ○ Legal Guardian

Living? ○ Yes ○ No (Date deceased _____)

Home address **if different** from yours

_____

_____

_____

Home phone (_____) _____
        Area Code

E-mail _____

Occupation _____

Name of employer _____

College (if any) _____

Degree _____ Year _____

Graduate school (if any) _____

Degree _____ Year _____

Parent /Guardian 2 _____
          Last/Family   *First*   *Middle*   *Title*   *Gender*

○ Mother ○ Father ○ Legal Guardian ○ None

Living? ○ Yes ○ No (Date deceased _____)

Home address **if different** from yours

_____

_____

_____

Home phone (_____) _____
        Area Code

E-mail _____

Occupation _____

Name of employer _____

College (if any) _____

Degree _____ Year _____

Graduate school (if any) _____

Degree _____ Year _____

Parents' marital status: ○ Never married ○ Married ○ Widowed ○ Separated ○ Divorced (date _____)

With whom do you make your permanent home? ○ Parent 1 ○ Parent 2 ○ Both ○ Other _____

Please give names and ages of your brothers or sisters. If they have attended college, give the names of the institutions attended, degrees, and approximate dates. If more than three siblings, you may list them on an attached sheet.

Name/Relationship	Institutions Attended	Degree(s)	es

EXTRACURRICULAR, PERSONAL, AND VOLUNTEER ACTIVITIES (INCLUDING SUMMER)

Please list your **principal** extracurricular, community, and family activities and hobbies **in the order of their interest to you**. Include specific events and/or major accomplishments such as musical instrument played, varsity letters earned, etc. Check (✔) in the right column (PS) those activities you hope to pursue in college. **To allow us to focus on the highlights of your activities, please complete this section even if you plan to attach a résumé.**

Activity	Grade level or post-secondary					Approximate time spent		Positions held, honors won, or letters earned
	9	10	11	12	PS	Hours per week	Weeks per year	

ACADEMIC HONORS

Briefly list or describe any scholastic distinctions or honors you have won since the ninth grade (e.g., National Merit, Cum Laude Society).

_____

_____

_____

WORK EXPERIENCE

Please list principal jobs you have held during the past three years (including summer employment).

Specific nature of work	Employer	Approximate dates	Approximate # of hours spent per week
_____	_____	_____	_____
_____	_____	_____	_____
_____	_____	_____	_____
_____	_____	_____	_____
_____	_____	_____	_____

SHORT ANSWER

Please briefly elaborate on one of your activities (extracurricular, personal activities, or work experience). Attach your response on a separate sheet (150 words or fewer).

PERSONAL ESSAY

This personal statement helps us become acquainted with you in ways different from courses, grades, test scores, and other objective data. It will demonstrate your ability to organize thoughts and express yourself. We are looking for an essay that will help us know you better as a person and as a student. Please write an essay (250–500 words) on a topic of your choice or on one of the options listed below. **Please indicate your topic by checking the appropriate box below.**

○ ❶ Evaluate a significant experience, achievement, risk you have taken, or ethical dilemma you have faced and its impact on you.

○ ❷ Discuss some issue of personal, local, national, or international concern and its importance to you.

○ ❸ Indicate a person who has had a significant influence on you, and describe that influence.

○ ❹ Describe a character in fiction, a historical figure, or a creative work (as in art, music, science, etc.) that has had an influence on you, and explain that influence.

○ ❺ A range of academic interests, personal perspectives, and life experiences adds much to the educational mix. Given your personal background, describe an experience that illustrates what you would bring to the diversity in a college community, or an encounter that demonstrated the importance of diversity to you.

○ ❻ Topic of your choice.

Attach your essay to the last page on a separate sheet(s) (same size please). You must put your full name, date of birth, and name of secondary school on each sheet.

OTHER REQUIRED INFORMATION

① Have you ever been found responsible for a disciplinary violation at any secondary school you have attended, whether related to academic misconduct or behavioral misconduct, that resulted in your probation, suspension, removal, dismissal, or expulsion from the institution? ○ Yes ○ No

② Have you ever been convicted of a misdemeanor, felony, or other crime? ○ Yes ○ No

If you answered yes to either or both questions, please attach a separate sheet of paper that gives the approximate date of each incident and explains the circumstances.

I authorize all secondary schools I've attended to release all requested records and authorize review of my application for the admission process indicated on this form.

_____   _____
Signature   Date

APPLICATION FEE PAYMENT   ○ Check/money order attached   ○ Counselor-approved Fee Waiver attached

REQUIRED SIGNATURE   Your signature is required whether you are an ED, EA, REA, or regular decision candidate.

I certify that all information in my application, including my Personal Essay, is my own work, factually true, and honestly presented.

_____   _____
Signature   Date

IF APPLYING UNDER AN EARLY PLAN (1) Complete the Optional ED/EA/REA Declaration for your early application only. (2) Submit the Common Application ED/EA/REA form if the college requires one. (3) Understand that it is your responsibility to report any changes in your schedule to the colleges to which you are applying.

The Common Application, Inc., and its member colleges are committed to fulfilling their mission without discrimination on the basis of race, color, national origin, religion, age, sex, gender, sexual orientation, disability, or veteran status.

     © 2006 The Common Application, Inc.

that it was a tough act to follow when I showed up with blueberry muffins. Kelli learned quickly that while in some ways her roommates were a few rungs above her financially, socially, and personally, they were delightful friends that she would come to trust and enjoy. She learned a lot about designer handbags and clothing that year.

Our youngest son's roommate from Hawaii, of Chinese descent, proved to be the most respectful and reverent of all our kids' roommates, and they talked percussion from the moment they met at the University of North Texas. At first, Ryan's roommate was a bit private and "way too neat." But eventually, the long conversations about life in Hawaii and his family helped Ryan to realize his roommate's life experiences and aspirations, while different from his own, were just as valuable. Even though Ryan eventually transferred, he keeps in touch with his first roommate.

So the moral of these stories goes like this: Be open to new people and new experiences and begin to let go of what is comfortable and familiar, and your college experience will be off to a great start. Taking a roommate from home with you to college may be comfortable and reassuring but it may not allow you to grow as you wish. It has been said many times that your high school friends will always provide memories but it will be your college friendships that transition into lifelong relationships. Open the door.

In fact, be open to a new invention that some colleges have created: *living/ learning* or *residential college.* These programs offer the benefits of living in a dormitory with other students who have similar interests, creating a unique culture of their own. In these living situations, it is common for a lecture to be held in the residence-hall common room for students by their professors, on a topic that all students would be interested in. These lectures are often inclusive of dinner, lecture, and then afterward, informal conversations with the professor. Many private universities that are currently providing living/learning situations are Yale University, the University of Miami, Rice University, and Baylor University. Public universities offering the program are the University of Michigan, UC San Diego, UC Santa Cruz, the University of Illinois at Urbana-Champaign, the University of Massachusetts, UNC Chapel Hill, and the University of Wisconsin at Madison. Take advantage of this opportunity if your college offers it. You will not only meet people that are interested in your major, you will have the extra enrichment that can only come when professors meet with you and talk about your field on a very personal level.

As for the application itself, below are some questions often found on a typical housing request. See how your preferences are addressed in the questions.

Please state your nationality.

How would you describe your lifestyle? (conservative, liberal)

Do you have a smoking preference?

What are your study habits?

Do you prefer a tidy room or does it matter to you if it is messy?

HOW TO SAY IT

I would suggest that you write down specific information if you like things rather orderly and need time to study such as the following statement:

I prefer to study between 6 p.m. and midnight. I need a quiet setting, although I do like to listen to rock music with headphones at times. I consider myself to be honest and somewhat respectful. I have three sisters so I know how to share. I would like an honest roommate that enjoys having fun but knows when to be serious.

Good luck!

Financial Aid Applications: Sign Up Early or Else!

There's a good chance that many of you have parents that started saving for college the day you were born. There's the rest of you whose parents did not start saving then, but are ready to help pay for college through installment plans. Still the rest of you may have a situation that requires scholarships, grants, and student loans. No matter what your situation, apply for financial aid. The money is there, waiting for you.

Each year thousands of students don't apply and miss out on free money. "The American Council on Education, which represents colleges and universities, says that half of the 8 million undergraduates enrolled at institutions participating in federal student aid programs did not complete the main federal aid application form" (The Associated Press, October 12, 2004). Apparently many of those students assumed that they wouldn't get aid because they wouldn't qualify. Everyone qualifies. How much a student gets, however, depends on two things: (a) need and (b) timing. The application has to be completed *early* in February . . . I am talking February 1! Most colleges cut off any FAFSA applications as of April 1. If you haven't applied by then, you won't get financial aid of any kind, unless the college you choose is extremely flexible and wants you desperately. But don't hold your breath for that. When the clock starts ticking after February 1, the money starts dwindling as well. Be on time.

The FAFSA, which can be completed online, is the *first and most important step* in applying for grants and scholarships (you don't pay those back) and *student loans* (which do have to be repaid). The form runs about four pages and each year seems to be getting simpler. What you will need to fill out the FAFSA:

1. Your parents' W-2 forms from their employers, which every employer is required to give to their employees by January 31.

2. Your W-2 forms from your employer, if you have a job.

3. Your mother and father's Social Security numbers and their addresses if they live in different places.

4. The full names of your siblings and their grade status in school, particularly if one or more attend college.

5. Information about your savings or bank accounts, your parents' savings accounts and whether they own any other assets.

This year it is estimated that about 9 million students will receive some sort of financial aid award. Become one of the recipients! I strongly suggest that you start filling out the FAFSA on your own, fill in what you know, save it, and then ask your parent(s) to sit down next to you to complete the portions that require information from them. Once completed, you can either sign it and mail it or request a FAFSA PIN. Once you receive a PIN, you can submit the application electronically every year. Program the PIN into your cellular phone for future use. You will need to reapply for financial aid every year and the PIN will make the process go much faster.

The FAFSA administrators will respond through e-mail that they received your application. They will also send the FAFSA application back if you need to add additional information. Until the FAFSA is completed, your college cannot and will not gather any financial aid award together for you. It can be quite frustrating to call and ask how the process is going for the scholarship application that you filled out only to be told that until you complete the FAFSA, your application is on hold. That's why it is very, very important to get it in early—very. Think of it as the big 5K college race for money. Whoever gets the application in first, gets their chance at the big bucks.

Another online application for nonfederal financial aid is *PROFILE*, the financial aid application service of the College Board. It is helpful to apply to both PROFILE and FAFSA since many colleges use either one, and the PROFILE is used by individual institutions to configure their own money for your needs. There are a few other differences between the PROFILE and the FAFSA:

1. Application deadlines: You can submit the PROFILE beginning October 1 for the following fall. The FAFSA can't be submitted until January 1.

2. The PROFILE will ask you more specific questions about the school you are choosing to attend or the major you plan to study.

3. Each of the applications determines your financial needs in a different manner, taking into account the assets your family owns.

4. The PROFILE requires that you, the student, contribute some money toward your education. The FAFSA does not.

5. The PROFILE allows the financial aid staff at a college to take more liberty in giving you financial aid because the questions asked on the application are more personal. If you have had a hardship in the past, for example, that can contribute to getting more aid.

6. The PROFILE costs $5 plus $18 for each school or scholarship program that you apply to. The FAFSA is free.

One last word about the costs of private versus public universities: Don't narrow your college choices because of college costs. A private college that charges $27,000 a year for tuition and room and board may hand out an average financial aid package of $18,000. The cost of a public university where the tuition may run $10,000 a year for tuition, room, and board may first appear much less expensive, but if you subtract the grants and scholarships given at a private university from the total bill, you may find that attending the private university is a possibility. Of course, you can also apply for financial aid through the FAFSA at the public university, which can yield more savings. So, don't let the cost scare you at first . . . do the FAFSA and sit back to see what the colleges offer. If you prefer one school over the other but dislike the financial aid offer, call the financial aid department and try to negotiate by using the following letter as an example:

HOW TO SAY IT

I have received an admissions letter to your college, which was my first choice. But, the financial aid package that you gave me is lower than the one I received from _____ University and may keep me from attending your university. I would like to see if you could review my financial aid application again and see if I would be eligible for more funding. It will make the difference in which university I attend, and I would really like to attend yours.

Many students are able to negotiate a better award package by this method. While e-mail is an easy way to converse with the financial aid office, I suggest a phone call so that the person on the other end can hear the sincerity in your voice and your desperate hope to attend their college. This is the beginning of a life where you pursue your dreams. Do it with vigor and "rigor."

"I Can Guarantee You a Scholarship . . . Just Give Me Your Credit Card"

If anyone approaches you or your parents trying to sell you life insurance or telling you that he/she knows some connections that will guarantee you a scholarship . . . run, run, run.

A legitimate scholarship search website or even a company representative *will never ask you for money*. So, don't pay anyone anything for scholarship information or for applying for a scholarship. If you follow the information in this chapter and apply early and on time to the FAFSA and or the PROFILE, your chances are the best they can be in the way of scholarships, grants, and student loans. Every year people pay money to scholarship scams that never pay out. Instead of looking for additional scholarship "guarantees," other than the PROFILE or FAFSA, look at www.fastweb.com, which lists thousands of scholarships that you can write essays or answer questions about to apply. You will never pay a fee at www.fastweb.com. There is no easy street to getting scholarships, but you can stay smart by filling out your applications early and remembering this info.

College Trivia Quiz #5

My name used to be Lew Alcindor and I played basketball for UCLA in 1967, then went on to play for the NBA. I changed my name. What is it?

a) Muhammad Ali
b) Kareem Abdul-Jabbar
c) Dick Nemelka
d) Don May

College Clues and Cues

There is a myth among freshman students that during the first year of college, students gain "the freshman fifteen"; that is, fifteen pounds. However, a recent survey published in 2002 by the *Journal of American College Health* has confirmed that only 59 percent of college students gained weight during their freshman year and the average amount put on was 4.6 pounds, less than one-third of the dreaded freshman fifteen.

It makes sense that as you move into a new environment, experience new activities, do more of this, do less of that, stay up later, study more (and more), and spend a lot of time exploring, that your diet and body will change. But you can prevent the feared myth by taking a few simple precautions:

1. Stay active. If you were involved in sports in high school, don't stop now. You will probably see students on in-line skates, skateboards, bikes, and in running shoes everywhere. Become one. You might be surprised who you meet.

2. Avoid the vending machines. To do this, stock up on fruit, which is often available at your college bookstore, dorm, or cafeteria. If you can keep good stuff handy, you won't go wandering at 11 p.m. for a chocolate fix to keep you going on your biology assignment.

3. Eat three meals a day. Chances are that you are paying for a meal plan. Eat it. If you skip breakfast and then load up on food later, it may stay with you and creep on as extra weight. If you eat too much breakfast and not lunch or dinner, you may be a bit sleepy midmorning. So, eating three times a day on a busy schedule will keep food running through your system and provide you with all it takes to think and concentrate.

4. Drink water. Not that I want to sound like your mother, who is soon to be far away, but if you drink a glass of water prior to each meal,

you will eat only what you need. Water has been proven to hydrate our brain, helping it to function better. It's often free, and always calorie-free.

5. Watch out for emotional eating. If you aren't used to staying up until very late to study, you may find yourself starving around 11 p.m. If this happens, check out when you ate last and see if it is stress that is rumbling in your tummy instead of hunger. If it's stress, take a walk, lift weights, go talk to a friend, or call home. Get a tall glass of water and get back to the books.

College Clues and Cues
For Parents

Maybe you thought he would miss you. Instead, the phone isn't ringing. When you call, his roommate says he is out and that he will give him the message. Or, you keep getting the recording on his cell phone. He only calls once per week. How could he forget all that you have done for him? Doesn't he know that you miss him?

Launching a teenager into college isn't as much fun for parents as the college brochures indicate. Smiling faces, waving good-bye to their perfectly capable offspring is often not the case. Instead, there are usually tears of joy and sadness all mixed up with the boxes and suitcases. Things will never be the same. But that's the good news! They will become more mature, eventually, and make better decisions.

No matter what, there may be a time, late at night, about three to four weeks into the first semester, as reality settles in, when you get a phone call:

"Mom, I don't know how to study. I didn't do well on my first quiz and I have another one tomorrow. What if I don't pass? Maybe college is not a good idea for me. I miss my friends, my brother, and my dog. Can I come home?"

To which you should wipe your tears, stop smiling (he misses us!), sit up straight, think of the tuition you are paying and how you have reached your offspring before. Plus, this time, add some understanding, self-disclosure, and belief that things will get better:

"You know, just the other day I was thinking how proud of you I was that you chose to go away to college. I didn't go away to school. I waited until I graduated to move. I missed everyone, too, just like you. It's a change. But I believe you can do it.

"I remember when you started high school and had a rough time trying out for the football team. Do you remember what you did? You practiced and practiced and you didn't give up. Then there was the time in your junior year when you wanted to be class officer and some people ran against you that you felt you couldn't beat. Remember how amazing it was when you won?

"I know you wonder right now if you made the right choice and I hope you figure out that it was. But for now, tell me what you learned about the last quiz. Tell me what you think you should study tonight for tomorrow's quiz.

"I will get your brother to e-mail you tomorrow . . . he's been a little swamped with his middle school science project. I know he will be anxious to write to you. I will also tell Dad that you called and get him to e-mail you, too. He'll be back from his business trip tomorrow. Until then, go study, know that I love you and believe in you.

"Call me tomorrow after the test."

As you express your belief in your offspring, you reignite his belief in himself. What he doesn't need from you is advice. He needs to figure out things for himself. By observing how he was successful in other situations, you bring back fond memories and memories of success. These words will give him something to sleep on and perhaps the next time you hear from him, you will hear a happier tone in his voice.

Your Profile of Courage: How to Get the Best Recommendations

*What lies behind us and what lies ahead of us are tiny matters
compared to what lives within us.*
—Ralph Waldo Emerson

The following letter of recommendation is one that might be sent by a teacher on behalf of a student to a particular college/university. As you read through it, try to imagine what kind of college setting the student is applying to.

> *Dear Admissions Staff,*
>
> *It is my pleasure to recommend Susie Senior to your school as a candidate for admission. Susie has exhibited excellent academic skills throughout her high school years, beginning her senior year with a GPA of 4.2. As a member of the National Honor Society and as class president of her senior class, she exemplifies what our school district refers to as a natural leader.*
>
> *Susie informed me that since her elementary school days in Girl Scouts, she has enjoyed being part of a team that made a difference.*

This was evident as she partook in a variety of community service activities during her middle school and high school years. Recently, she volunteered to travel with a youth group to work with Hurricane Katrina victims and when she returned, she joined local organizations to further the relief through clothing drives and food banks.

In addition to all of these fine qualities, Susie has a wealth of friends who seem to support her endeavors. In a typical class such as my AP English class, Susie often rises to the occasion to debate an issue that she feels passionate about yet knows when to sit back and listen to her classmates respectfully. She has the integrity and compassion to speak up for causes that she believes in, yet realizes that others have their own opinions.

I have also spoken to her basketball coach, who confirmed that she is able to do the pull-ups that you require, the forty-yard sprint, a mile run, and shoot a basketball from her knees.

Please consider Susie Senior as an applicant for admission to your freshman class. It is my professional opinion as her English teacher that she would add to the class and become a team member that everyone would enjoy knowing.

Sincerely,
Kim Gallant, Teacher

This is a letter of recommendation to the United States Military Academy. In addition to a letter such as this, which mentions academic, leadership, and physical attributes, this student would also have to obtain a congressional recommendation, and a recommendation by two senators and the vice president of the United States. The congressman may request that the student fill out a form so that he/she can write a recommendation that is flattering to the student. The student may also have to interview with the congressman before a letter is written. Captain Bryan Pinedo also mentioned the following good advice to students applying to the USMA:

This is a long process and if you are thinking about it you should begin working toward this goal in your first year of high school. Build relationships with your teachers and community leaders that will help you when they write the letters. Volunteer in political things so you can get to know your congressmen. Keep your grades up, protect your reputation, and stay physically fit so you can pass the physical exam. Volunteer for things and take on leadership roles. Leadership is looked at and is important. Leadership abilities, grades, character, work ethic are all considered.

While most of the colleges that you apply to won't require you to shoot basketballs from your knees, the ideas expressed in regard to the student in this letter are important to think about. By volunteering, staying physically fit by participating in sports, dance, cheerleading, ROTC, and participating in any other activities inside or outside of school, you not only improve your health, you show your appreciation for a variety of activities that make you "well rounded." Also, take on any leadership role that you can. Many of the schools that were interviewed for this book focused on the importance of seeing such roles on their applications because it means the student is a self-starter that can complete college classes successfully.

So let's get started with the recommendation process.

First, Plan (Again) and Get Organized

Organization is the key to making sure your recommendations get written and mailed to where they need to go on time. First, using the College Fact Sheet (in the appendix), make a copy for each college that you want to apply to and write the name of the college at the top of the page. Then write down who you are going to ask to write your letters of recommendation for that particular college along with the following information:

- Application deadline for admission.

- Application requirements such as sending test scores, transcripts, essays.

- Specifics about your letters of recommendation such as who needs to write them and deadlines for when the letters should arrive.

Next, copy off enough Recommendation Letter Request forms (in the appendix) for everyone that you are going to ask to write a letter and address two envelopes:

- Envelope #1: Address this envelope to the college and add a stamp.

- Envelope #2: Address this envelope to yourself and add a stamp. The person that writes the recommendation letter can write down the date that the letter was sent on the Recommendation Letter Request form and mail it to you. This way you know it has been sent. Teachers and school counselors are busy people. This will keep them accountable to you as it will remind them when the letter has to be in and if they forget, you can remind them.

Fill in the information and when you are finished, make a copy for your own safekeeping. This way, if you don't hear back from the person who you asked to write a letter of recommendation, you can visit them again with a gentle reminder. Use the College Contact Sheet to keep track of what's happening and what's been finished.

Deciding Who to Ask

Think of teachers and school staff that know you well. Particularly choose teachers who have seen you perform well, not just academically but socially and as a team member. For example, if you were someone that often debated issues in a particular class in a thoughtful manner and the teacher noticed your participation, ask that teacher for a recommendation. Other teachers can comment about your academic skills and talents in classes such as art, drafting, or family sciences class.

If you helped an associate principal out with student council activities or the special education teacher with tutoring other students, ask them for a recommendation. Additionally, a recommendation letter from the superintendent or principal that you met when you were engaged in a sports tournament is always appreciated and impressive.

Other people to consider are people that you worked with in your job, church, outside sports, or community events. For example, if you volunteered at a hospital during the summer vacation, and met a physician that seemed to take an interest in you, ask the physician for a letter of recommendation, particularly if you are interested in the medical field. If you want to be a high school coach and you played football for several years in high school, ask your coach for a letter.

Don't forget another obvious source of excellent recommendation letters . . . alumni. Nothing says it better than an alumni who recommends you for the same university that they attended. The admissions staff assumes that the recommender knows the type of student that the university profiles when he/she attended the same school.

Finally, ask your employer for a letter of recommendation, particularly if you have worked for the same employer for at least six months. Your ability to be on time and do a good job is something employers can describe best. As Roz Bolger, a former admissions officer at Emory University says, teachers, peers, and employers "know the students in ways we can't. They can tell us about the student's character and how they've seen them grow."

Check out on the college website or in the application materials how many letters of recommendation the college requires. Some schools require more than one and even if the school only requires two, send three or four.

The only people that I don't encourage you to ask are your family members. Let's just say they might be biased! While their credibility is high with you, their comments won't be nearly as credible to an admissions staff member.

Timing Is Everything

It is best to begin approaching people for letters of recommendation around early November. Teachers and school counselors are busy people and the beginning of the school year is quite hectic, as is the last part of the school year. Ask those people that you want to write a letter for you for an appointment after school or during their break. Take the following with you to give to them:

1. Experience Worksheet

2. Résumé

3. Recommendation Letter Request form

4. A Format for Recommendation Letters

5. Envelopes (as described above . . . one for you, the other for the school, both stamped)

What If They Ask You What to Write?

"The best recommendations give some insight about the student and knowledge of the school the student is applying to," says Chris Boyle, senior associate director of admissions at Knox College in Galesburg, Illinois. He encourages students to take time to explain to the recommenders what majors they are interested in studying and to explain why they have chosen the particular college. It is also helpful to explain why the student chose the particular person for a recommendation letter. Flattery works in this situation, quite well.

HOW TO SAY IT

Many people will ask you what to write. That typically means that they are willing to write more than a "form recommendation letter." This is your cue to sit down with the recommender for a few minutes and tell them why you are applying to Best University:

"I really appreciate your asking me what to write. I do have some ideas from the university in regard to what they want that I can tell you about."

Then, tell the recommender what you hope to major in and also share why you chose him/her to write the letter. Mention positive experiences with him/her. Perhaps you want to major in English and you chose your AP English teacher. It would make sense to say:

"I chose you to write my letter because I enjoyed your class and having you as my teacher. You gave me assignments to do that took a lot of time but in the end, I learned a lot. It made me very interested to go on and become an English teacher."

Look out for alums! Perhaps you know of an alumnus that attended Ohio State, the university you are applying to. To them you can say:

"I know that you attended Ohio State and that you go back to attend a football game every year to watch the Buckeyes. I have always liked your enthusiasm for the school so it influenced me to apply there. I think it would be a good fit for me and I like their Zoology major."

Letter of Recommendation Format:
The Importance of Appearing "Unique"

Since you are almost a high school graduate, let's test your observation skills. Read the following letter of recommendation and find the error:

HOW *NOT* TO *EVER* SAY IT!

Dear Admissions Staff,

It is my pleasure to recommend Susie Senior for admission to Ohio State University. I have known Susie for three years, and during that time I have had her in two of my classes, biology and AP biology, where she was a stellar student. Not only did she earn As in both classes, she joined the biology club and has participated in a variety of experiments that the club sponsored during the past two years.

Susie possesses excellent study habits and takes the initiative on projects and assignments. She is a good group leader and team member. In addition, she often helped tutor freshman biology students after school as part of the National Honor Society duty, of which she was a member.

Susie has discussed why she wants to attend Iowa State University and I commend her on her choice. I know that she will make a valuable contribution to your university as a student and a community leader. Please consider accepting Susie Senior.

Sincerely,

Imada Mistake

Biology Teacher, Best High School

Did you find the mistake? If not, look again. What school is Susie Senior applying to? Ohio State or Iowa State? This is what happens too often, according to the admissions staff at Boston University. And, when it does, what kind of credibility do you think Imada Mistake has with the staff? How do you avoid this disaster? Talk to your recommenders and ask them to focus, if possible, on your unique qualities. While you can't look over their shoulder while they write the letters, if the recommenders offer to let you read it before they mail it, take them up on it and check for an error. You can even give them a format to follow, like the form below. This form is reproduced in the appendix so you can copy it off and hand it to the person writing the letter.

HOW TO SAY IT

A FORMAT FOR RECOMMENDATION LETTERS

Paragraph #1: Recommend the student for admission to the university. Write about the number of years that you have known the student and in what capacity.

Paragraph #2: Discuss the student's activities academically and any other activities that contribute to the student's character. Mention unique qualities about this student that separates the student from other applicants. Write about personal experiences that you had with the student in regard to academic diligence and success. Mention how these assets will serve the student well throughout her college career. Add comments on your confidence that this student will succeed in the major that she has chosen to study.

Paragraph #3: Give your professional opinion about this student and recommend her for admission to the university. Mention how the student will add to the campus community and how she will be a prosperous student that will represent them well in the future.

Forms, Forms, and More Forms

In addition to letters of recommendation, the Common Application includes two Teacher Evaluation forms that you will print out and hand to two of your teachers. Samples of those forms start on page 138. Notice how the first one is called Teacher Evaluation 1 and the second, Teacher Evaluation 2. This is how the colleges will keep track of your forms and how you can keep track of who mailed the form in. Fill in the information that is requested at the top of the first page, sign it, make a copy, and on the copy, write down the teacher's name that you will be giving the form to. This will keep you organized. Put the copy with the College Fact Sheet. It will be helpful to get a file folder or a pocket folder where you can keep things together for each college.

Look through the evaluation form and then notice that the last page is a "ratings" page. Notice all of the different assets that your teachers will need to rank you on. To help them with this, it may be helpful to get a copy of your high school transcript so that they can review your grades before they rank your abilities. Choose two teachers that you have a good rapport with as well as a good academic record. The ratings portion of the evaluation form focuses on how mature, confident, kind, persistent, disciplined, productive, and of course, intelligent you are. Take time to show the recommenders the Experience Worksheet. It will give them more insight into the kind of student and person that you are.

Sports Recommendations

Maybe you liked participating in sports so much that you want to do it again in college. While your coach will have a lot to say about you on his/her letter of recommendation, unfortunately he/she can't get you a spot on the team. There are, however, some things that you *must* do in order to participate in college sports, such as sign up for the NCAA Clearinghouse.

The NCAA Clearinghouse is located in Iowa City, Iowa, and is the organization that handles all questions regarding a student's eligibility to play college sports. The Clearinghouse has a website that you need to look over, www.ncaaclearinghouse.net.

Registering for the Clearinghouse will also make you eligible for receiving athletically based financial aid. To register, you need a Social Security number and a Visa or MasterCard, because there is a fee. If you have a Visa debit card, that will work as well. If you got a fee waiver for the SAT or ACT exam, you can request one for the Clearinghouse as well, but your registration will not be processed until your high school sends in the waiver confirmation, so remind your school counselor (the person to ask about the fee waiver on all accounts) to send it quickly.

You will need to request that your school send the Clearinghouse official transcripts and test scores. If you have been homeschooled at any time, there

2006-2007
TEACHER EVALUATION

The member colleges and universities fully support the use of this form. No distinction will be made between this form and a college's own. Please type or print in black ink. Be sure to follow the instructions on the cover page of the Common Application booklet to complete, copy, and submit your application to one or more of the member institutions.

TO THE APPLICANT

After completing all the relevant questions below, give this form to a teacher who has taught you an **academic** subject (English, foreign language, math, science, or social studies). Please also give that teacher stamped envelopes addressed to each institution that requires a Teacher Evaluation.

Birth date _____   Social Security No. _____
        mm/dd/yyyy   *(Optional)*   ○ Male
Legal name _____   ○ Female
*Enter name **exactly** as it appears on passports or other official documents.* *Last/Family*   *First*   *Middle (complete)*   *Jr., etc.*

Address _____
        Number and Street   *Apartment #*   *City or Town*   *State/Province*   *Country*   *Zip/Postal Code*

School you now attend _____   CEEB/ACT code _____

> **IMPORTANT PRIVACY NOTICE:** Under the terms of the Family Education Rights and Privacy Act (FERPA) you WILL have access to your recommendation after you matriculate UNLESS at least one of the following is true:
>
> 1. The institution does not save recommendations post-matriculation *(see list at www.commonapp.org/FERPA)*.
> 2. You waive your right to access below:
>
> ○ Yes, I *do* waive my right to access, and I understand I will never see this recommendation.
> ○ No, I *do not* waive my right to access and may someday choose to review this recommendation.
>
> ✎ _____   _____
> *Signature*   *Date*

I authorize all secondary schools I've attended to release all requested records and authorize review of my application for the admission process indicated on this form.

✎ _____   _____
Signature   *Date*

TO THE TEACHER

The Common Application membership finds candid evaluations helpful in choosing from among highly qualified candidates. A photocopy of this reference form, or another reference you may have prepared on behalf of this student, is acceptable. You are encouraged to keep the original of this form in your private files for use should the student need additional recommendations. Please return it to the appropriate admission office(s) in the envelope(s) provided you by this student. Please submit your references promptly. **Be sure to sign on the reverse.**

BACKGROUND INFORMATION

How long have you known this student and in what context?

_____

_____

What are the first words that come to your mind to describe this student?

_____

_____

List the courses you have taught this student, noting for each the student's year in school (10th, 11th, 12th; first-year, sophomore; etc.) and the level of course difficulty (AP, accelerated, honors, IB, elective; 100-level, 200-level, etc.).

_____

_____

_____

SAMPLE

Please detach along perforation

RATINGS

Compared to other students in his or her class year, how do you rate this student in terms of:

No basis		Below average	Average	Good (above average)	Very good (well above average)	Excellent (top 10%)	Outstanding (top 5%)	One of the top few encountered in my career
	Academic achievement							
	Intellectual promise							
	Quality of writing							
	Creative, original thought							
	Productive class discussion							
	Respect accorded by faculty							
	Disciplined work habits							
	Maturity							
	Motivation							
	Leadership							
	Integrity							
	Reaction to setbacks							
	Concern for others							
	Self-confidence							
	Initiative, independence							
	Overall							

EVALUATION

Please write whatever you think is important about this student, including a description of academic and personal characteristics, as demonstrated in your classroom. We welcome information that will help us to differentiate this student from others. (Feel free to attach an additional sheet or another reference you may have prepared on behalf of this student.)

SAMPLE

Teacher's name (Mr./Ms./Dr., etc.) _____ Title _____
                                                    Please print or type

Secondary school _____

School address _____
                    Number and Street   *City or Town*   *State/Province*   *Country*   *Zip/Postal Code*

Teacher's phone (_____) _____ Teacher's e-mail _____
                Area Code   *Number*   *Ext.*

✎ _____   _____
           Signature   *Date*

THE COMMON APPLICATION
For Undergraduate College Admission

2006-2007
TEACHER EVALUATION

The member colleges and universities fully support the use of this form. No distinction will be made between this form and a college's own. Please type or print in black ink. Be sure to follow the instructions on the cover page of the Common Application booklet to complete, copy, and submit your application to one or more of the member institutions.

TO THE APPLICANT

After completing all the relevant questions below, give this form to a teacher who has taught you an **academic** subject (English, foreign language, math, science, or social studies). Please also give that teacher stamped envelopes addressed to each institution that requires a Teacher Evaluation.

Birth date _____ Social Security No. _____
　　　　　　 mm/dd/yyyy　　　　　　　　　　　　　　　　　　　　 *(Optional)*　　　　　　　　　　○ Male
Legal name _____ ○ Female
Enter name exactly as it appears on passports or other official documents. Last/Family   First   Middle (complete)   Jr., etc.

Address _____
　　　　 Number and Street   Apartment #   City or Town   State/Province   Country   Zip/Postal Code

School you now attend _____ CEEB/ACT code _____

IMPORTANT PRIVACY NOTICE: Under the terms of the Family Education Rights and Privacy Act (FERPA) you WILL have access to your recommendation after you matriculate UNLESS at least one of the following is true:

1. The institution does not save recommendations post-matriculation *(see list at www.commonapp.org/FERPA).*
2. You waive your right to access below:

○ Yes, I *do* waive my right to access, and I understand I will never see this recommendation.
○ No, I *do not* waive my right to access and may someday choose to review this recommendation.

_____ _____
Signature　　　　　　　　　　　　　　　　　　　　　　　　　　　　　 *Date*

I authorize all secondary schools I've attended to release all requested records and authorize review of my application for the admission process indicated on this form.

_____ _____
Signature　　　　　　　　　　　　　　　　　　　　　　　　　　　　　 *Date*

Please detach along perforation

TO THE TEACHER

The Common Application membership finds candid evaluations helpful in choosing from among highly qualified candidates. A photocopy of this reference form, or another reference you may have prepared on behalf of this student, is acceptable. You are encouraged to keep the original of this form in your private files for use should the student need additional recommendations. Please return it to the appropriate admission office(s) in the envelope(s) provided you by this student. Please submit your references promptly. **Be sure to sign on the reverse.**

BACKGROUND INFORMATION

How long have you known this student and in what context?

_____
_____

What are the first words that come to your mind to describe this student?

_____
_____

List the courses you have taught this student, noting for each the student's year in school (10th, 11th, 12th; first-year, sophomore; etc.) and the level of course difficulty (AP, accelerated, honors, IB, elective; 100-level, 200-level, etc.).

_____
_____
_____

RATINGS

Compared to other students in his or her class year, how do you rate this student in terms of:

No basis		Below average	Average	Good (above average)	Very good (well above average)	Excellent (top 10%)	Outstanding (top 5%)	One of the top few encountered in my career
	Academic achievement							
	Intellectual promise							
	Quality of writing							
	Creative, original thought							
	Productive class discussion							
	Respect accorded by faculty							
	Disciplined work habits							
	Maturity							
	Motivation							
	Leadership							
	Integrity							
	Reaction to setbacks							
	Concern for others							
	Self-confidence							
	Initiative, independence							
	Overall							

EVALUATION

Please write whatever you think is important about this student, including a description of academic and personal characteristics, as demonstrated in your classroom. We welcome information that will help us to differentiate this student from others. (Feel free to attach an additional sheet or another reference you may have prepared on behalf of this student.)

Teacher's name (Mr./Ms./Dr., etc.) _____ Title _____
Please print or type

Secondary school _____

School address _____
Number and Street   _City or Town_   _State/Province_   _Country_   _Zip/Postal Code_

Teacher's phone (_____) _____ Teacher's e-mail _____
Area Code   _Number_   _Ext._

✎ _____
Signature   _Date_

TE-2 / **2006-2007**   **TEACHER EVALUATION 2**   © 2006 The Common Application, Inc.

THE COMMON APPLICATION
For Undergraduate College Admission

2006-2007 SCHOOL REPORT

The member colleges and universities fully support the use of this form. No distinction will be made between this form and a college's own. Please type or print in black ink. Be sure to follow the instructions on the cover page of the Common Application booklet to complete, copy, and submit your application to one or more of the member institutions.

TO THE APPLICANT

After completing all the relevant questions below, give this form to your secondary school counselor or another school official who knows you better. Please also give that school official stamped envelopes addressed to each institution that requires a School Report.

Birth date _____   Social Security No. _____
mm/dd/yyyy   *(Optional)*   ○ Male
Legal name _____   ○ Female
Enter name exactly as it appears on passports or other official documents. Last/Family   First   Middle (complete)   Jr., etc.

Address _____
Number and Street   Apartment #   City or Town   State/Province   Country   Zip/Postal Code

Current year courses—please indicate title, level (AP, IB, advanced honors, etc.) and credit value of all courses you are taking this year.

First Semester/Trimester   Second Semester/Trimester   Third Trimester

_____   _____   _____
_____   _____   _____
_____   _____   _____
_____   _____   _____
_____   _____   _____
_____   _____   _____

Please detach along perforation

IMPORTANT PRIVACY NOTICE: Under the terms of the Family Education Rights and Privacy Act (FERPA) you WILL have access to your recommendation after you matriculate UNLESS at least one of the following is true:

1. The institution does not save recommendations post-matriculation *(see list at www.commonapp.org/FERPA)*.
2. You waive your right to access below:

○ Yes, I *do* waive my right to access, and I understand I will never see this recommendation.
○ No, I *do not* waive my right to access and may someday choose to review this recommendation.

_____   _____
Signature   *Date*

I authorize all secondary schools I've attended to release all requested records and authorize review of my application for the admission process indicated on this form.

_____   _____
Signature   *Date*

TO THE SECONDARY SCHOOL COUNSELOR

Attach applicant's official transcript, including courses in progress, a school profile, and transcript legend. (Please check transcript copies for readability.) After filling in the blanks below, use both sides of this form to describe the applicant. Please provide all available information for this candidate. **Be sure to sign on the reverse.**

Class rank: _____ in a class of _____, covering a period from _____ to _____
(mm/yyyy)   *(mm/yyyy)*

The rank is ○ weighted ○ unweighted. How many students share this rank? _____

○ We do not rank. If a precise rank is not available, please indicate decile _____.

Cumulative GPA: _____ on a _____ scale, covering a period from _____ to _____
(mm/yyyy)   *(mm/yyyy)*

This GPA is ○ weighted ○ unweighted. The school's passing mark is _____.

Highest grade/GPA in class _____   Graduation date _____

Percentage of graduating class attending: _____four-year _____ two-year institutions

© 2006 The Common Application, Inc.

Are classes taken on a block schedule?
○ Yes ○ No
If yes, in what year did block scheduling begin?
_____

If you offer AP courses, do you limit the number a student can take? ○ Yes ○ No

In comparison with other college preparatory students at our school, the applicant's course selection is:
○ most demanding   ○ demanding
○ very demanding   ○ average
                              ○ less than demanding

SR-1/**2006-2007**

RATINGS

Compared to other students in his or her class year, how do you rate this student in terms of:

	No basis	Below average	Average	Good (above average)	Very good (well above average)	Excellent (top 10%)	Outstanding (top 5%)	One of the top few encountered in my career
Academic achievement								
Extracurricular accomplishments								
Personal qualities and character								
Overall								

EVALUATION

Please write whatever you think is important about this student, including a description of academic, extracurricular, and personal characteristics. We welcome a broad-based assessment that will help us to differentiate this student from others. (Feel free to attach an additional sheet or another reference you may have prepared on behalf of this student.)

How long have you known this student and in what context? _____

What are the first words that come to your mind to describe this student? _____

_____

① Has the applicant ever been found responsible for a disciplinary violation at your school, whether related to academic misconduct or behavioral misconduct, that resulted in the applicant's probation, suspension, removal, dismissal, or expulsion from your institution? ○ Yes ○ No

② To your knowledge, has the applicant ever been convicted of a misdemeanor, felony, or other crime? ○ Yes ○ No

If you answered yes to either or both questions, please attach a separate sheet of paper or use your written recommendation to give the approximate date of each incident and explain the circumstances.

○ Check here if you would prefer to discuss this over the phone with each admission office.

I recommend this student: ○ With reservation   ○ Fairly strongly   ○ Strongly   ○ Enthusiastically

Counselor's name (Mr./Ms./Dr., etc.) _____
                                        Please print or type

✎ _____
Signature   *Date*

Title _____   School _____

School address _____
                    City or Town   *State/Province*   *Country*   *Zip/Postal Code*

Counselor's phone (_____) _____   Counselor's fax (_____) _____
                   Area Code   *Number*   *Ext.*   *Area Code*   *Number*

Secondary school CEEB/ACT code _____   Counselor's e-mail _____

                                            © 2006 The Common Application, Inc.

THE COMMON APPLICATION

For Undergraduate College Admission

2006-2007 MIDYEAR REPORT

The member colleges and universities fully support the use of this form. No distinction will be made between this form and a college's own. Please type or print in black ink. Be sure to follow the instructions on the cover page of the Common Application booklet to complete, copy, and submit your application to one or more of the member institutions.

TO THE APPLICANT

After completing all the relevant questions below, give this form to your secondary school counselor or another school official who knows you better. Please also give that school official stamped envelopes addressed to each institution that requires a Midyear Report.

Birth date _____
mm/dd/yyyy

Social Security No. _____
(Optional)

○ Male
○ Female

Legal name _____
Enter name _exactly_ as it appears on passports or other official documents.   Last/Family   First   Middle (complete)   Jr., etc.

Address _____
Number and Street   Apartment #   City or Town   State/Province   Country   Zip/Postal Code

> **IMPORTANT PRIVACY NOTICE:** Under the terms of the Family Education Rights and Privacy Act (FERPA) you WILL have access to your recommendation after you matriculate UNLESS at least one of the following is true:
>
> 1. The institution does not save recommendations post-matriculation _(see list at www.commonapp.org/FERPA)._
> 2. You waive your right to access below:
>
> ○ Yes, I _do_ waive my right to access, and I understand I will never see this recommendation.
> ○ No, I _do not_ waive my right to access and may someday choose to review this recommendation.
>
> ✎ _____
> Signature   Date

I authorize all secondary schools I've attended to release all requested records and authorize review of my application for the admission process indicated on this form.

✎ _____
Signature   Date

TO THE SECONDARY SCHOOL COUNSELOR

Current year courses—please indicate title, level (AP, IB, advanced honors, etc.) and credit value of all courses this student is taking this year.

First Semester/Trimester	Second Semester/Trimester	Third Trimester
_____	_____	_____
_____	_____	_____
_____	_____	_____
_____	_____	_____
_____	_____	_____

If your recommendation for this student has changed since the School Report was submitted, please comment in the space below or on a separate sheet of paper. If nothing has changed, you may leave this section blank. However, your signature is required on the reverse.

Attach applicant's official transcript, including courses in progress, a school profile, and transcript legend. (Please check transcript copies for readability.) After filling in the blanks below, use both sides of this form to describe the applicant. Please provide all available information for this candidate. **Be sure to sign on the reverse.**

Class rank: _____ in a class of _____, covering a period from _____ to _____
(mm/yyyy)   _(mm/yyyy)_

The rank is ○ weighted ○ unweighted. How many students share this rank? _____

○ We do not rank. If a precise rank is not available, please indicate decile _____.

Cumulative GPA: _____ on a _____ scale, covering a period from _____ to _____
(mm/yyyy)   _(mm/yyyy)_

This GPA is ○ weighted ○ unweighted. The school's passing mark is _____

Highest grade/GPA in class _____   Graduation date _____

Percentage of graduating class attending: _____ four-year _____ two-year institutions

Are classes taken on a block schedule?
○ Yes ○ No
If yes, in what year did block scheduling begin?
_____

If you offer AP courses, do you limit the number a student can take? ○ Yes ○ No

In comparison with other college preparatory students at our school, the applicant's course selection is:
○ demanding
○ most demanding   ○ average
○ very demanding   ○ less than demanding

© 2006 The Common Application, Inc.

MR-1/**2006-2007**

RATINGS

If any of the information in this section has changed for this student since the School Report was submitted, please enter the new information in the appropriate space below. If nothing has changed, you may leave this section blank.

Compared to other students in his or her class year, how do you rate this student in terms of:

No basis		Below average	Average	Good (above average)	Very good (well above average)	Excellent (top 10%)	Outstanding (top 5%)	One of the top few encountered in my career
	Academic achievement							
	Extracurricular accomplishments							
	Personal qualities and character							
	Overall							

EVALUATION

If your recommendation for this student has changed since the School Report was submitted, please comment in the space below or on a separate sheet of paper. If nothing has changed, you may leave this section blank.

SAMPLE

If any of the information below has changed for this student since the School Report was submitted, please enter the new information in the appropriate space below. If nothing has changed, you may leave this section blank. However, you must print your name and sign below.

① Has the applicant ever been found responsible for a disciplinary violation at your school, whether related to academic misconduct or behavioral misconduct, that resulted in the applicant's probation, suspension, removal, dismissal, or expulsion from your institution? ○ Yes ○ No

② To your knowledge, has the applicant ever been convicted of a misdemeanor, felony, or other crime? ○ Yes ○ No

If you answered yes to either or both questions, please attach a separate sheet of paper or use your written recommendation to give the approximate date of each incident and explain the circumstances.

○ *Check here if you would prefer to discuss this over the phone with each admission office.*

I recommend this student: ○ With reservation   ○ Fairly strongly   ○ Strongly   ○ Enthusiastically

Counselor's name (Mr./Ms./Dr., etc.) _____
Please print or type

✎ _____
Signature   *Date*

Title _____ School _____

School address _____
            City or Town   *State/Province*   *Country*   *Zip/Postal Code*

Counselor's phone (_____) _____ Counselor's fax (_____) _____
        Area Code   *Number*   *Ext.*   *Area Code*   *Number*

Secondary school CEEB/ACT code _____ Counselor's e-mail _____

© 2006 The Common Application, Inc.

will be a section to fill out. If you attended high school in the United States and will graduate from one, you will fill out the Domestic Student Release form. If you attended a high school outside of the United States, you will fill out the Foreign Student Release Form. The point of all this information gathering is to, again, make you eligible for financial aid.

Stats Can't Guarantee You Will Play

If you apply for a sports scholarship or to play in college, your high school coach will be asked by the college to provide information. While the coach can give you high marks on your sports career in high school, the coach won't say whether or not you should be recruited. But, you can request that your coach look over the résumé that you will compose at the end of this chapter, and from that, write a recommendation commending you on a variety of assets. If you recall the list from the U.S. Military Academy at the beginning of this chapter, the assets on that list are always of interest to colleges because in addition to wanting a great team, the colleges also want you to graduate.

When college coaches look at evaluations, recommendations, and films, they look more for potential than success during high school and they also look at how you come across when you meet the coaching staff face to face. "You have guys that are just good high school football players, but not everyone is a recruitable athlete on the college level," Tennessee State University football coach James Reese said. Colleges tend to have large budgets for recruiting football and basketball players, whereas other college sports have smaller budgets. Because of this, if you want to play these two sports, your high school coach may have more of a role in getting you noticed by a college. If you are interested in sports that are not as competitive such as softball or swimming, your high school coach may be able to call up the school that you want to play for and get you recruited just from a phone call.

The last chapter of this book focuses on interviewing skills. Look over some of the tips before you meet and greet your potential new coach.

Fine Arts: Art, Drama, Dance, and Music Recommendations

Naturally, if you have won art contests, exhibited your work in community libraries, or received an award, you will want your art teacher to send in an evaluation and or a letter of recommendation. To help your art teacher, tell her/him how often you create work at home, and how long you have been interested in art as a career. This will help to again create a list of assets that the colleges will notice. Hopefully you have a teacher who can help you to compile a portfolio of your best work. Go to an art store and buy a huge portfolio folder and fill it with items that you are the most proud of. This is particularly helpful if you transferred from one high school to another before you graduated. By showing your teacher the work you are proudest of, you will refresh his/her memory before the recommendation letter is written.

If you were in orchestra, marching band, or any other ensemble and participated in UIL contests, region contests, or even national contests, make sure that you list those achievements on your Experience Worksheet, and later on your college application. Do this even if that means you add an additional pages. List the following:

Name and describe every contest you participated in.

Name and describe the awards and scores that you received during the contests.

State how many years you were involved in musical activities.

State how often you practiced and how loyal you were to committing to summer or after-school practices.

Describe your dreams for the future in music.

If you began acting or dancing in a community theater at age eight, put that down on your résumé. If you designed some scenery for a play in eighth grade,

College Trivia Quiz #6

This very famous musician is the eldest of eight children, the daughter of an engineer father and housewife mother. At a young age she signed up for any artistic outlet she could find such as school shows, the cheerleading squad, piano lessons, and ballet classes. Her dancing skills were so advanced they earned her a scholarship to attend the University of Michigan. While she did not finish her college career, she made her mark there and on stage worldwide. Who is she?

a) Beyoncé Knowles
b) Madonna
c) Britney Spears
d) Christina Aguilera

jot it down. Mention how many plays you have participated in even if it involved small parts. Include newspaper clippings that were written about you and your talent as part of your application and photocopy them to give to your drama or dance teacher to review as he/she writes the evaluation or recommendation letter.

Hopefully if you are planning on becoming a media major of any type, whether it be film, journalism, or photography, you will have already begun compiling a portfolio. A portfolio should be a representation of your best work. Get a notebook with clear sheet protectors to put your valuable articles or photos in. If your work is film, compose a "reel" (ask your media tech teacher to help you do this) and get it on DVD so that teachers can review your work. Make it your best work since how you put it together will definitely be an indicator of your current skill level. You can use this portfolio to describe your abilities to your recommenders and to include in your college application.

Recommend Yourself! The Résumé

Just when you thought the compilation of experiences was over, you have one more request from the college that relates to recommendations: a résumé. Today, more colleges are asking for résumés as they convey quickly the assets of the applicant. The following sample résumé is an example of using the right action verbs, the right adjectives, and a nice format.

Susie Senior
1234 Yellow Brick Road
Perfect City, California 90210
323-123-4567

EDUCATION

Beach High School, Perfect City, California
Diploma expected June 2007
GPA: 97.21%

LEADERSHIP

Beach High School

- Student Council Treasurer, 2004
- Student Council Secretary, 2005
- PALS—A peer mediator, 2005-2007
- Journalism Club President, 2007

Trinity Methodist Church

- Youth Group Chairman—Ski Trip, 2005

EMPLOYMENT

Perfect City News Journal

- Wrote teen column for college bound teens.
- Gathered clippings for advertising department.

COMMUNITY Service

Perfect City Animal Shelter

- Provided 300 hours of community service during 11th and 12th grade as part of a volunteer program of the student council to contribute to the community.
- Instructed 2nd-grade special education students who needed tutoring at the Shale Elementary School in Perfect City, California, after school during the 12th grade.

SKILLS/INTERESTS

Proficient in Spanish
Computer literate
Interested in animal rights and legislation
Interested in teaching students with mild learning disabilities

- References Available Upon Request

The following résumé template is the one that was used to build Susie Senior's résumé. It will help you to put together your experiences and educational efforts. You will find it useful to use not only for college purposes but for job applications now and in the future. I suggest that you keep it on your flash drive and your PC or laptop as a permanent file and add to it as you finish high school and you enter college. After you enroll in college, revisit the résumé every time you join a club, sorority, fraternity, academic activity, or participate in anything on campus, including a part-time job. It is easy when you are a senior to overlook activities that you did when you were a freshman or sophomore. You are building a résumé of your life work. Keep track of it.

Refer to the list of action verbs in this chapter as well as the adjective list to confidently recommend yourself in your résumé. Put together phrases like Susie Senior did that explain your activities and your assets and skills.

Résumé Template

Fill in *your* information wherever there are italics.

Full Name (First, Middle, Last)
Address
City, State, Zip Code
Telephone (and area code)
E-mail address (if applicable), website (if applicable)

EDUCATION
- *Name of high school attended, community college attended (for dual-credit classes)*
- *Degree awarded: major and/or minor (high school diploma)*
- *Date degree to be awarded (date of graduation)*
- *GPA, if 3.5 or above*
- *Off-campus study/study abroad*

LEADERSHIP

- *List all school offices held*

Example: Student Council Treasurer

Decorations Committee—Prom

Journalism Club—Secretary

Key Club—Animal Shelter Representative

- *List any other offices or positions of leadership outside of school*

Example: Youth Group Chairman—Howard Baptist Church

Karate Instructor—Assigned after receiving black belt

Teen Court member, Fall 2005

EMPLOYMENT

- *Position title, organization name—Example: Office Depot*
- *City and state where organization is located, dates of service*
- *Description of skills used*

Example: Provided customer service, which included informing customers about different technologies that would be useful in their home or office. Contributed to the development of a method of copying large orders for a local company so that job turnaround time was decreased.

VOLUNTEER/COMMUNITY Service

- Example: Provided 100 hours of volunteer time to the Johnson City Homeless shelter as part of a volunteer project sponsored by the student council.
- Example: Worked with the Johnson City homeless shelter to devise a method of organizing clothing for teenagers who are in need.
- Example: Assisted an elementary teacher by providing tutoring for students through the PAL program, a division of FFA.

AWARDS & HONORS

- Example: Received black belt in Karate, June 5, 2005
- Example: Member, National Honor Society
- Example: Senior Award: Highest GPA in Mathematics

SKILLS (if applicable)

- Example: Speak Spanish
- Example: Computer literate
- Example: Experience in video editing with Vegas software

References available upon request.

College Clues and Cues

Once you are on campus, you may begin to notice sorority and fraternity jerseys everywhere. Being a part of the social scene via a fraternity or sorority "club" will provide you with instant friends . . . sisters or brothers for life. The parties and events will be fun and exciting and there's nothing like the lifelong memories and friendships that you will make together. But before you join, do yourself a favor. Instead of trying to figure out what the letters mean, keep your eyes and ears open about the various clubs, the kind of students they recruit or "*rush*," and the reputation of the club.

To do so, begin asking classmates or dorm buddies what they know or have heard about the clubs you are interested in. Are they known for "hazing," being a club for jocks, or for too much partying? Are they known to be "good girls" who make good grades and are community volunteers? What is the required GPA to rush and be a member? Find out when the meetings are and what is required of members. Find out the costs. Dues for fraternities and sororities can range from $200 a semester to $800 a semester. Then there are the pin, the rush fee, and the application fee which may require you to get former members to recommend you before school ever starts. Some clubs won't even consider you without a recommendation. *Legacy* plays a small part in being invited to join a club these days, but no longer is it a given that you will be invited to join if your mother or father was a member. It's up to you to make a great impression, which in many ways is better as it means you will be accepted based on your personality, not on who your parents are.

Take your time to rush. The first semester that you attend college is stressful enough. If you "pledge" a club the first semester, you are opening up yourself for more work and the possibility that your academics might suffer. If possible, wait until spring or fall of your sophomore year when you know the ropes of the campus, you know the reputations of the clubs, and can make a better decision. Many students that pledge during their freshman year often go inactive by their junior year just because they tire of the countless activities and demands on their time. It seems a better option to wait until your grades are on track to add another activity such as pledging. And when you do decide, look forward to belonging to a group that will follow you for the rest of your life. You will always be someone's sister or brother with memories to share.

College Clues and Cues
For Parents

If you pledged a sorority or fraternity while in college, chances are that you remember the fun and the friendships, some of which you may still have today. As a parent, however, the scope changes when you begin thinking of your son or daughter joining a club, particularly when you are paying tuition that seems to drain the bank each semester. And then, maybe you have memories of some wild and crazy times, too. That's rather scary.

To put your worries to rest, there are a few things that are different about the sororities and fraternities today. For the most part, for example, they promote academic excellence. To even rush, a candidate must have a GPA of at least 2.5 in most cases, and for some, 3.0. Plus, the students that join the club must keep the GPA to stay a member. Additionally, there are study hours and tutoring programs that many clubs adopt to promote their reputation as good students.

Then there are the parties. To drink or not to drink won't even be a question, it will be a culture. By now, you have probably relayed your views on underage drinking and explained the hazards of binge drinking to your teen. While you won't be there to monitor, the campus Panhellenic chair will have certain regulations that all clubs must adhere to for the most part and they will be different for all campuses. To relieve your mind further, check with the Panhellenic chair by calling Student Services and inquiring about any recent problems with club activities in relation to alcohol or drugs. Also inquire about hazing and ask how it is monitored on the campus. Relay your information to your son or daughter. While he/she may see you as overprotective, if you give the information as just that, information and not as a lecture, ending it with the following questions, you may score some points on the "cool parent" scale.

HOW TO SAY IT

Begin with: "I am so proud of you. I know you are excited about going to college and I wanted to share some things about belonging to a sorority or fraternity. I know you will make a decision based on careful thought."

"I'm interested in what kind of sorority you are attracted to."

"Tell me what you are looking for in a fraternity?"

"What do you think would indicate that a club was/wasn't right for you?"

"If you saw a group of students hazing another or making a student do something rather weird, what do you think would be the right thing to do?"

"What is your opinion about binge drinking?"

End your conversation with an open plea of "You know, I will miss you next year but I want you to have a great time. If anything comes up that you want to talk to me about, I promise not to lecture and instead, I will just listen to you. I always want you to know that I believe in you and that you will make some good decisions."

Things are going to change between your son and daughter and yourself, but don't let that thing be communication. Keep the doors and phones and mailbox open for their complaints and trials as well as their excitement. Be their consultant, not their lecturer. Help them make new decisions based on what they want to achieve, not on what you want them to achieve.

7

Essay Writing 101: Telling It Your Way

Ryan Rose Weaver, BS, Emerson University, 2006

What I like in a good author isn't what he says,
but what he whispers.

—*Logan Pearsall Smith*

Four years after I entered college, I made an appointment to talk with the admissions director at my school. I was early and sat waiting, anxiously—I felt like I was in a secret headquarters, where major life decisions are made, and stone-faced counselors in business suits cackle humorlessly over the hapless efforts of eighteen-year-old essayists, tossing them by the thousands into a heap of white paper.

Instead, I watched as two staff members, both in their twenties and dressed in jeans and sandals, teased one another over the top of a computer screen. Then, suddenly, I saw them chasing after each other down the hallway. One kicked over a garbage can. It was an incredibly silly scene. And I thought to myself: *These kinds of people once helped to determine my fate? They're normal, just like me.*

When I entered the admission director's office, I prepared myself to meet a sharp-jawed, no-nonsense woman, given to marching applicants out of her office if they used improper grammar. Instead, I found a ruddy-faced, friendly, blonde thirty-something woman inside, who listened to my questions about this book and answered them with respect and often a quick laugh. She beamed as she recalled the best essays she had ever read: people who took chances, made jokes, and bared their souls. And I thought to myself: *This person is behind the scary admissions process? She's a nice woman—just like me.*

Had I known that caring individuals made up each and every admissions staff, I might have relaxed a bit when writing my essays. The audience you picture for yours will make a big difference in its tone and overall effect.

I know of a radio station director who had hired a new crop of disc jockeys, and had begun to hear them say very strange things and use tones of voice on-air that were not like their everyday voices at all. After all, DJs tend to be very outgoing, friendly people. So he called them into a room one by one and asked them to describe the audience they were picturing when they stepped up to the mike.

One answered, "A faceless group of thousands of people that I can't see." Others pictured disapproving relatives or parents who were older than they were who might be listening, while still others believed that their audience likely knew much more about music than they did and would never listen to their station again if they made a mistake. So of course when they went on air to talk to these critical, judgmental authority figures, or worse, a frightening crowd of people they could not see, they sounded formal and fake or nervous and defensive.

He encouraged them to picture the ideal listener (a person very much like the actual listeners of the station according to their polls): a kind, open-minded person who looked to them for inspiration, knew them to be friendly and fun, and would likely forgive their limited shortcomings. He also pointed out that many people who listen to the radio are alone or in pairs, and so a broadcast should sound as if it were a conversation with one or two people, not tens of thousands. Not surprisingly, the new DJs were able to loosen up and sound like themselves again—funny, likeable human beings.

So, when you go to write your essay, you should not begin by thinking it will be sent off to a faceless organization that might view your essay cynically or reject you outright. Instead, you might picture an admissions person much like a favorite aunt or cousin who is not that much older than you, who enjoys reading what you write and who wants to help you succeed. For ten or fifteen minutes, you will have a conversation with this one person where you will tell them about yourself and why they should respect you.

Pretend that you will make the admissions counselor's day if you can impress them with your skills and your story—one he or she hasn't already read on your résumé. Let the real you come through: the writer, the painter, the biker, the hiker, the big sister or brother, the devoted daughter or grandson, the loyal friend, the passionate activist, the entrepreneur-in-training—all of the things that impress real people like you, me, and your admissions counselor.

Getting Started! Essay 101

Describe yourself in five hundred words or less: the most difficult challenge and most important opportunity you will face on your application. While your transcript and SAT scores are now out of your control, the college essay is a chance for you to tell counselors something they won't find in those stark numbers and letters: It allows them to hear your voice. With questions that ask you to describe your biggest challenges, relate your proudest accomplishments, or describe your favorite fictional character (we're not kidding here), counselors are trying to help you break out of the standardized, laundry-list-of-accomplishments mindset that you've been trained to live by for the past four years. They want to know what your family is like, what you do after school, how you spend your weekends, what dreams keep you up at night. They also want to know how they and the school they represent can help you to make those dreams a reality.

In a way, this essay will be an easy one to write: you don't have to spend hours in the library researching it, or suffer through a boring book or film in order to learn about the subject. The subject is you, and you are the expert on it. And you won't have to stay up late agonizing over the number of pages: At only 400 to 500 words (approximately one typewritten page), you may worry about running out of space instead.

The essay may also be one of the most challenging things you will write, because you can't fall back on previous research on the subject (you're the first and only you). You can't talk about the subject objectively because you're living out the history behind it every day, so you may not be able to see trends in your actions clearly. You may have so many different areas of interest that it's tough narrowing down one thing to talk about. You may procrastinate until the last minute because you are too busy to think about anything other than what's going on right now with school, work, friends, and family. You may also feel that you have "writer's block"—a condition brought on by the anxiety of writing that keeps you from coming up with ideas and putting them down on the page. You may also struggle with your English skills, spelling, or voice. You may wonder: If I don't often sound like *me* when I write, how can I bare my soul to strangers? This chapter will give you some tips and tricks to get around some of these obstacles.

One thing I *can't* tell you is how to make your essay sound like anyone other than you—an eighteen-year-old student reflecting on your last few years of high school and relating your dreams about the years to come. No one can write this essay for you, and you shouldn't try to sound like anyone else as you write it. Just remember that no matter what college you're applying to, you'll be able to complete the essay effectively if you follow the tenets of all good writing:

- write what you know

- know your audience

- do your research

- organize your essay carefully and follow directions

- use stylish but earnest language

- follow proper grammar principles

- edit for the greatest effect

Keep in mind that despite the fact that the essay will be a short, original composition by you, preparing to write a successful essay will take more time and preparation than you'd think. Try not to write it at the last minute. This chapter will guide you through the steps necessary, but make sure that you follow its guidelines. You should give yourself a few weeks to a month to complete this process. You will need to do the following:

- properly brainstorm ideas

- research your prospective schools

- review the essay question for each school

- write one or more drafts of your essay that meet the word counts and criteria requested by each school

- edit carefully, ideally with the help of a parent or teacher

Write What You Know!

Take a breath and relax: This essay is not going to ask you to explain the Krebs cycle of photosynthesis, or why the symbolism in *The Scarlet Letter* shows the conflict between nature and civilization. You won't need to wait to receive a transcript, a letter, or even help from your parents to begin this assignment. You have everything you need already. This is because the most common kind of essay question is one that in one way or another asks you to tell your life story. A good example is this year's essay question for incoming Columbia students. Here is the prompt:

> *Write an essay which conveys to the reader a sense of who you are. Possible topics may include, but are not limited to, experiences which have shaped your life, the circumstances of your upbringing, your most meaningful intellectual achievement, the way you see the world—the people in it, events great and small, everyday life—or any personal theme which appeals to your imagination. Please remember that we are concerned not only with the substance of your prose but with your writing style as well. We prefer that you limit yourself to approximately 250–500 words (Columbia University application, 2006–2007 school year).*

This question has several components and seems very open-ended—there are a lot of ideas here that might inspire you to open up about yourself. Just think—after all these years that your parents taught you not to brag, you can finally talk about how great you are. But how do you collapse the last eighteen years of "experiences that have shaped your life" into 500 words? They must be crazy!

Here's how. First, give yourself about two weeks to brainstorm topics you might tackle in this essay. Take a break from *doing* and think about *why* you do what you do. In this section, there are three kinds of ideas that you can use for inspiration:

- **Write down a list of your biggest accomplishments and biggest challenges.** How do they relate to each other?

- **Work backward: imagine your dream life after college.** Why did you choose that dream? How will your college of choice play a role in making it come true?

- **Interview the "experts."** Ask friends and family to tell you a story about yourself. What do they think are the best examples of your maturity, intelligence, creativity, or selflessness?

Use the Experience Worksheet . . . Again!

This method is the most straightforward way to developing your essay, because it contains the information you'll need to answer almost every essay question posed by any school. To begin, look at your Experience Worksheet that you filled out earlier. Where are your biggest strengths? What activities did you become involved in because they reflected the real you? Did you join an environmental group because you've always loved camping? Did you start a business helping others your age? Don't forget to write that down, even if you slide it under "Extracurricular Activities."

The next part is equally as important. Look at your Experience Worksheet and résumé again and ask yourself: What *doesn't* it say about me? What's missing in the story it tells? Is your GPA or your SAT score lower than you'd like? Is your list of activities or your course load coming up short? Think about why you made the decisions that led to these results—like most people, maybe you likely had other things to worry about besides creating lines on that piece of paper. Did you cut back on challenging classes to play a sport you loved, or cut back on school activities to free up hours for your part-time job? Did you forego taking a challenging class because of an illness or a learning disability? Did you stay in a difficult course despite the lower grades you'd receive because you really wanted to master the material? Did you struggle through an important semester due to problems with money or family issues?

For example, while in high school, my list might have looked like this:

Summer 2000: Moved across the country. Sat alone in the cafeteria for my first week at a new school. Joined as many clubs and teams as possible to transition into life in a new state and meet people. (Was later voted Prom Queen my senior year because of the many committed friendships I had made.)

Fall 2000: Didn't make tennis team. Got part-time job instead with caterer. Helped to support myself and my single mom by making money and learning to cook.

Spring 2001: Didn't make softball team. Learned how to play lacrosse; went on to start on varsity team the following year and met my best friends on the team.

Fall 2001: Came down with mononucleosis. Spent a month in bed. Had to drop out of AP Chemistry. Took AP Biology the following year, applying what I had learned. Got a 5 on the test.

This list isn't any longer than half a page (and you will be able to make yours a bit longer than that), but it represents the bulk of what I thought a college should know about me. It shows that I started high school behind the eight ball, coming from a completely different place, and added a wide range of activities to my résumé only after I became adjusted to my new home. It explains that I came from a lower-middle-class family and had to spend more hours at work than my other friends, so I didn't belong to every club at school—but that I learned valuable lessons there as well (like managing my time and learning to cook) that would help me to transition into adulthood during my college years because I had to take on adult responsibilities. And most of all, it shows that I had already pulled up my roots and started over in a new place once before, and it was clear that I had managed to not only compete with but surpass my peers in accomplishments and maturity as a result, so I would be able to do the same when I moved 400 miles away to begin college.

Think about the ways that you can explain your life and your decisions— or the things that were out of your control that you turned to your advantage. Most admissions counselors are interested in that side of you—because while grades measure everyone on the same scale, there are many different ways to value a whole person and their strengths, whether they include "emotional intelligence" in dealing with family and friends or "street smarts" that help you to survive tough situations outside of school. These character traits might be something you took for granted—something you "had" to do. But they have been "experiences that have shaped your life" in a way that your chemistry class last year probably wasn't, and are more appropriate material for an essay.

So now, you may be ready to try this exercise yourself. Write down the biggest obstacles you've experienced—and overcome—during your high school years—and they should not all be academic in nature.

The best times were . . .

_____

_____

_____

_____

The worst times were . . .

_____

_____

_____

Now, look at your lists. You may think that your first list—the one that lists your strongest points—is where you should begin when you write your college essay. You should sell yourself as well as you can using your good grades and awards, right? Not always!

College admissions officers have access to your résumé like anyone else, your high school counselor will send them your course schedules and grades, and the College Board will make sure they see your SAT scores, for better or for worse. When you only have a page or less to tell your story, it's imperative that you don't waste space telling colleges what they already know about you!

A bad example of a college essay would read like this:

I think that I would be good material for UC Berkeley because I won the state science fair in 2003. I have been winning science fairs since I was in second grade. I was a member of the U.S. First Robotics team for three years, and I took third place in 1999, second place in 2000, and second place in 2001. I was a member of Science Olympiad during my junior and senior year, and acted as its vice president. We won the national competition in September of my senior year. I was also a member of National Honors Society, a prestigious national organization, for three years of high school. I acted as its treasurer during my junior year . . .

Now, what does this tell us about the student? Nothing that we can't read on the résumé and nothing about the kind of person he is. But what if it read like this?

Sample Essay #1

Ever since I was small, I remember being interested in the way things worked. My father, who worked as a car mechanic for most of my life, spent his days pulling the wires out of old cars, then came home and pulled the wires out of old computers. He was fascinated with new technology and always handed me a pair of pliers so I could "help" him figure it out. When I found out about my first science fair in second grade, I think he was more excited than I was. We built my very first model: a tiny roller coaster that demonstrated gravity, made from my Erector Set. From there the bug infected me permanently. Every year when it started to snow and other kids were grumbling, I knew it meant one thing: science fair season.

There's a stereotype about science kids—that we're all introverts. But I loved talking shop with other kids like me, and I'm pretty outgoing—me and my dad both have a huge, booming laugh that makes my mom jump in surprise every time. So I joined any group I could: the U.S. First Robotics competition, where we got to visit a new city every year when we went to nationals; Science Olympiad, where we worked in teams to figure out problems. I ended up becoming a leader of both of these groups because I loved coming up with new ideas and strategies to help all of us succeed.

It wasn't always easy, though. When my dad came down with multiple sclerosis during my sophomore year, I felt like my limbs froze up, too: One day, his strong hands would lose the ability to hold a pair of pliers. For a while, I just wanted to stay home with him, and I withdrew from school: That year, I didn't do much besides homework and chatting with my dad, about all the inventions we made. But he told me that I'd be happier out with kids my age, talking about the big future ahead of us. I didn't like it, but he was right—I took all the energy I had and poured it into my inventions, and my group members respected my energy, which seemed unreal to them. One day I hope to create a machine that will help

MS patients with their symptoms. I think that the reputation UC Berkeley has for its great science organizations and its research will help me to do my best and to achieve this dream—for me, and for my dad. (Word count: 418)

This latter example shows several things that the former does not: It gives background to the student's genuine interest in science, showing that it wasn't just because he was pushed by his parents, but because it helped him grow closer with his father. It highlights his relationships with other people as well as his own interests. It shows why he is motivated to attend the specific school and that this choice matters to him. Most important, it paints a picture of a student who has not simply succeeded all of his life without obstacles; it shows that he has succeeded in spite of them and has relied upon his gift to help him through difficult times.

Not surprisingly, the Massachusetts Institute of Technology (MIT), one of the most prestigious engineering schools in the world, sees the benefit of asking their prospective students about these kinds of experiences. They know that it will allow students to describe their strongest resolve, commitment, and maturity, the qualities it takes to succeed in college. Their 2006–2007 admissions essay prompt reads as follows:

Tell us about an experience which, at the time, really felt like "the end of the world"—but had it not happened, you would not be who you are today. Describe the process through which you discovered value in the negative (Undergraduate Application, 2006–2007, Massachusetts Institute of Technology).

The author of this book, Linda Metcalf, is an expert on the idea of connecting future goals with past challenges: She wrote a book called *The Miracle Question* that asks readers to picture the thing that they most want—something that would be a miracle if it happened, like winning the lottery. She then asks them to trace their lives back to the times where they had something similar to the thing they wanted, like a time when they felt financially secure. After working through what made them feel successful and happy, the person has realized that they don't need a miracle in order to make it happen again; they just need to realize how the ways they've acted in the past have either helped or hindered them on their journey to reach their goals. She calls these situations "exceptions," a word that stands for the times when life worked better.

Similarly, achieving your goals in life—to become a doctor and help others, to become a teacher and work with children, to become a scientist and invent a revolutionary technology—will not be a miracle, but the sum of years of hard work and experiences during your childhood that have pushed you in that direction. But if you aren't sure how to show that to an admissions counselor, try working backward: telling them where you'd like to go, and what you have done in order to get there.

Working Backward to Go Forward

Imagine that tomorrow morning, you wake up ten years in the future—and you have your dream life. What profession will you be working in? What will your workday look like? With whom will you be working? What state or country will you live in? What will your house look like? What will make you most proud about your life? How will you feel (think about words like "successful," "helping others," "important," "secure," "triumphant")? Write the story of that day on a separate piece of paper.

What things are you doing that make you feel the same way—using the words you wrote down? What strengths do you already have that will help you to achieve that future life? Use the essay to tell the story of not only your past life, but your future dreams.

If you're still having trouble putting the last few years in perspective—and they've likely been busy ones—don't worry. This reflective process is difficult for everyone, whether they are eighteen or forty-eight. So try talking to the "expert sources" on the subject (which, remember, is you). Ask a parent, grandparent, best friend, or sibling to tell you a story about yourself that they think describes an important quality you possess. You may find that something small you've done has impacted them in a big way, that they've been impressed with the way you handled a situation when you simply thought you were surviving it, or that they can see a trend in the activities you've chosen that you hadn't. Their high opinion of you will help inspire you to talk about yourself in similarly glowing terms—sometimes it's easier to relate what other people have said about you than to say it yourself, and it will give your story credibility while showing the way you manage your relationships with others.

HOW TO SAY IT IN YOUR "INTERVIEW"

Questions to ask that get family and friends talking about you . . . to you!

"Can you tell me how I might have helped you to overcome a challenge?"

"When was the last time you thought I was really going to have a 'meltdown' because of a challenge or multiple challenges I faced, but then you saw me succeed anyway?"

"Would you tell me about a time that we really came together as a family over a challenge? How did I act in that situation that helped?"

"Would you tell me about a time when I acted most like an adult?"

"Would you describe a time when you were impressed by the way I solved a problem?"

"In what ways do I set a good example for others (siblings, relatives, friends)?"

"When have you seen me really excited about something? What words have I used to tell you why I liked the activity so much?"

"Would you recall a time when my support meant a lot to you? What about a time when you think your support meant a lot to me?"

"What admirable qualities do you see in me?"

"What is the most important thing you have wanted to teach me? Do you think that I have learned this lesson? In what ways do I show that?"

If you're still not sure what counselors will be interested in, don't worry. You're not a mind reader! So don't try to second-guess counselors—just talk to them. As we've discussed, counselors are looking not only for academic success but resounding proof that you'll be able to manage all aspects of living on your own. Below are a few imaginary "dialogues" between a counselor and student, with examples of what counselors might be thinking as they read the essays, and how students can illustrate the individual qualities that will make them well qualified to handle coming to college. Picture yourself in the student's shoes, and think about how you would handle these questions. Your essays should reflect who you are in the answers to the questions.

How confident are you in your ability to make decisions about your future? How will you go forward in each situation—whether it be changing your major, organizing a study abroad, or settling on a thesis topic— without having your parents there to talk it over with you, do the research, sign the forms, and pay the entrance fees?

Sample essay answer: When the manager offered me a job at the instrument shop, I hesitated. What would my parents think? They told me they wanted me to focus on school. But I knew that I would learn more about music—my true passion—and it would help me to become a better musician because I would be asked to know more about it. And the opportunity was waiting for me. I turned to him and said, "When can I start?"

How well do you manage your personal relationships? How will you get along with the two, three, four other roommates in your dormitory or

apartment, who instead of sending you to your room if you don't do your dishes or laundry (or doing it for you if you're too busy), are more likely to demand that you shape up or move out?

Sample answer: My two best friends have been fighting even before they met me. Donna thought Jenn's cheerleading was "stupid," while Jenn always ignored Donna, who she thought was "really dorky." And as my two best friends, they both fought over my time. But when I became so busy with school that I wanted to spend my limited time with both of them, I started inviting them both to our favorite mutual activities: football games, parties, and movies. At first they were suspicious of each other, but realized they had a few things in common—including me! Now the three of us do everything together, and they've helped each other to grow—Jenn has cracked down on her schoolwork, and Donna has really come out of her shell. I was proud of the way I didn't let petty differences stop us from enjoying ourselves and helped them to get over their differences. I know that at the all-girls school I'm applying to, this will come in handy!

How responsible are you for your needs? How much do you contribute to the upkeep of your household? How will you handle yourself when paying rent is added to your list of things to do before you sit down to your homework?

Sample answer: When my mom had to get an extra job to support our family, I made sure that my little brothers got dressed in the morning and had someone to help them with their homework at night. Because I helped my family to survive this transition, I feel confident that I will be the one to step up in future organizations—and after being responsible for others for so long, taking care of only myself will be a relief!

How well do you handle your responsibilities in a way that doesn't wear you down? How will you keep yourself focused and healthy without Mom or Dad putting dinner on the table every day and telling you when it's time for bed every night?

Sample answer: Because I was able to balance football practice with my regular responsibilities and it actually made me more focused, I realized the importance of maintaining both my body and my mind. When friends asked if I wanted to drink with them, I told them no—I had a big game in the morning. My teammates at the party saw my example and knew it was all right for them to say "no," too—Coach needed us to be at our best against our biggest rivals. I know now that while the pressure will be higher for me to say "yes" to unhealthy activities in college, the games will be even bigger. Because of what I've learned from this sport, I know that I will be able to keep my head in the game on and off the field.

Believe it or not, the way you handle "tests" like these is much more indicative of your ability to handle college life than your ability to take the SAT. Of course those scores are important and you have earned them, but counselors want to know that you've got what it takes in all of these areas. These are ideas that should come through in the words of your essay.

Know Your School

In addition to realizing you must impress an individual rather than an organization, it is also important that you recognize that the organization will determine what that individual will be looking for. It is important that you do some research about the institution to which you are applying. Each school wants to know why you are choosing them among the thousands throughout the country—it will help them to know why they should choose you.

The first place to look should be the college website. There are sections on every site for prospective students, where you can find profiles of current students, overviews of majors, credentials of professors, and—most important—the application itself, which is now online and downloadable in PDF form from almost every school in the United States Even better—they're available months in advance, with the fall season's applications available in early summer. Take advantage of this opportunity to read up on schools and read through each application's essay question. You should do this as early as possible, but no later than after your brainstorming process and *before* you begin to write. The application itself will often contain an introduction designed to acquaint the student with the school and the document, and contains important information about what the school expects from you. Take the time to tailor each essay toward the school's mission and focus—don't just copy and paste! Many counselors have stories of high schoolers who have used the same essay over and over, forgetting to omit the name of the last school they've applied to. If you send an essay to Northeastern expounding on how much you want to attend Ithaca, the counselor will wish you good luck—and move on to the next student.

To avoid missing the mark with your dream school, here are some questions you should answer with your research:

What's important to you?

In chapter 2, you read about the variety of majors, programs, and specialties that colleges offer. So if you're a soccer all-star, but wouldn't mind attending a Division III school because they have an excellent science program, you might want to talk more about your time behind the microscope than in front of the net. On the other hand, if you've chosen a school for its legendary athletics program and you're gunning for a scholarship, feel free to talk about the way teamwork taught you how to succeed beyond the soccer field.

What's important to your school?

Depending on what your school specializes in, admissions departments will have different priorities. If you are an excellent student from Turkey applying to be an engineer, your test scores may weigh more than your English skills in their decision. But if you are applying to a school with a strong communications and/or arts presence, be prepared to show your true colors in the essay. Admissions staff at these schools look closely not only at grammar usage and spelling but flair, style, pacing, and voice—and even a bit of chutzpah in the way a student handles this all-important question. Of course, if you have writing talent but are not applying to a writing program, by all means still let your creativity flow—colleges are looking for a well-rounded student. And no matter what program you are entering, there is always a chance to stand out with a story that makes you different from the other students in your program.

What major are you planning to declare, and why is this school's program the best place for your area of study?

What makes your dream school's program perfect for you, and why are you the right candidate to take one of the limited number of slots in it? Choose your words to suit the situation. Which says more about your ability to succeed as a film major—your lifelong passion for photography or your ability to pick out prom favors with the student council? If your goal is to be a brilliant advertising design major, which shows your artistic ability more convincingly, your membership in the National Honor Society or your collection of magazine collages at home?

What makes you excited about attending this school?

If you find yourself getting excited every time you learn something new about your college of choice, tell them why! Remember, counselors can only offer so many students the chance to attend their school—they want to make sure invitations are going out to students who really want to come. By showing enthusiasm about a specific school, you show that you have not just copied and pasted the same essay into each application, and that you will truly appreciate the acceptance letter they'll be sending you in the fall. It also means that you will be more likely to accept admission, and your adjustment to college life will be that much easier since you are already educated about the institution, minimizing the chance that you will transfer, leaving someone who might have loved it there out in the cold. When it comes right down to it, an admissions counselor's job is to act as a gatekeeper between you and your dreams. You want to make them feel good when they open the door for you by telling them the important role their college will play in making those dreams come true.

HOW TO SAY IT ABOUT YOUR SCHOOL

Because [your college of choice] is known for its strong [your prospective major] program, I'm really looking forward to taking my passion to the next level.

When I heard about [your prospective major], I knew that [your college of choice] would be the perfect place for me to learn the skills necessary to [name your long-term goal].

Because the alumni at [your college of choice] have gone on to succeed in [your chosen field], I am looking forward to joining your community.

After making a difference in my high school by [name accomplishment here], I am looking forward to bringing that sprit to your campus, which has a history of fostering social change.

After my [life-changing journey to favorite destination], I realized that I could only thrive in an environment like [your college of choice], which offers the same qualities [a beautiful setting, a thriving city, a diverse culture].

Tell Your Story with Honesty and Style

After you have come up with some ideas, drawn from your past experience and reflective of your school choice and future goals, and downloaded all of your applications, it's time to pen your first draft. You may want to divide your essay into the key components we've discussed—relating your background, expressing your current ability to perform in spite of challenges, and the role your chosen school will play in helping you to continue to succeed.

Remember that when you sit down to write an essay, you are getting ready to tell someone a story. Some parts are more interesting than others, and should be longer. Other details don't matter unless they are moving that narrative along to the conclusion. Try to develop your essay in a way that is compelling for the reader. Think about the best stories of our time. For example:

> Lance Armstrong, a famous cyclist, had talent beginning at a young age, becoming a triathlete at thirteen and a pro biker at sixteen. But his career was not an unfettered rise to the top: It was a series of advances and setbacks. He won the National Amateur Cycling Championship in 1991, but in 1992 he finished fourteenth at the Olympic Summer Games in Barcelona. The next year, he won the Pro Cycling Tour's Triple Crown. But in 1996, at the top of his game, his health began to deteriorate, and he dropped to twelfth place in the Olympic races. Then, he was diagnosed with cancer and his chances of racing again seemed nonexistent. But with chemotherapy and help from his friends, he went on to win six consecutive races.

Would you have cared about the Tour de France in 2005 if Lance "Livestrong" Armstrong hadn't been at the handlebars?

Think about how your story would read if it came complete with ups and downs, struggles and setbacks, accomplishments and triumphs. Look back at the list you made of your challenges and victories, and use that to make your story compelling.

HOW TO SAY IT: PARAGRAPH BY PARAGRAPH

Most essay word limits fall between 250 and 500 words. You should aim for an essay that is between 400 and 500 words, with an introductory paragraph that draws the reader into the story and three supporting paragraphs that address your background, current situation, and future goals. Therefore, as a guide, you may want to keep each paragraph within the bounds of 100 to 125 words, or a few short sentences.

PARAGRAPH 1: THE INTRODUCTION

You've heard it a million times: Your first paragraph should be a short, punchy sentence or two that gets the reader's attention. But this isn't a dry old assignment about a book that doesn't even interest *you*—this is an epic story about a very interesting person. Like the first few sentences of a news story, your story should start out with the most interesting, exciting detail . . . one that is sensory and concrete—your reader is almost there with you. Think about the details of your story: What you saw, heard, tasted, smelled, or touched that made one particular moment in the piece memorable. You may even want to write down the bulk of your essay first, then the introduction last, depending on what you discover as you are writing your story. But no matter what you write about, you want the essay reader, who may have read hundreds of other essays today, to wonder: What happens next? Here are two examples:

> **"I splashed into the cold water as the horn blared. I held my breath as I swam my first lap, as my teammates watched, holding theirs. You don't really know what responsibility means until you're charged with eliminating a tenth of a second—or the whole team loses."**
>
> **"I remember the first time I saw the birth of a calf, as I sat crouched in the hay of my grandpa's barn as a child. As I watched the veterinarian speak to the cow, I knew that I wanted to do the same thing when I grew up."**

Next comes the body of your piece, starting with a main paragraph that sums up what you'll be reading. This body could follow one of several formats.

TO DESCRIBE A LIFELONG PASSION:

Paragraph 2: *I first became interested in [your favorite activity] in [year]. When I started, I had no idea how to do [activity].*

Paragraph 3: *Now I have turned it into an opportunity to do [name accomplishments here].*

Paragraph 4: *I hope to [name goal here] during and after college.*

TO DESCRIBE A LIFE-ALTERING EVENT:

Paragraph 2: *Before [name hard time here], I was just like any other student.*

Paragraph 3: *Going through that situation made me realize that there was more to life than just good grades. I also had to help others who were in the same situation.*

Paragraph 4: *Because of [college of choice]'s reputation for promoting these ethics, I hope to make a change in the world.*

TO DESCRIBE A TUMULTUOUS JOURNEY:

Paragraph 2: *When I began to do [name activity here], everything seemed to fall into place—I loved it.*

Paragraph 3: *But then [name hard time here] happened, which hindered me in my goals. But in the meantime, I learned [describe lesson here], and when I returned to it, it was with more passion than ever.*

Paragraph 4: *Now I am more motivated than ever to put that to use at [name college here].*

TO DESCRIBE A SPECIAL TALENT:

Paragraph 2: *Ever since I was small, I loved to do [name activity here]. Everything I did centered on it—I ignored everything else.*

Paragraph 3: *Maybe I missed out some great opportunities, but I couldn't ignore my passion for [activity]. And while my friends have lots of awards and accomplishments under their names and I don't, I can [name ability here] better than anyone else I know.*

Paragraph 4: *Because [name college of choice] is known for doing that better than any other school, I know that I'll be happy there.*

Remember: You are getting these formats because it can be difficult to know how to organize your thoughts when the topics are often general and open-ended. But the best essays are ones where students have taken the format and used it to do something different, focusing on a moment that belongs to them alone. This is your chance to show your creativity: Make this essay the most original and authentic that it can be.

HOW TO SAY IT IF . . .

YOU'RE BETTER AT TELLING THAN WRITING

One way to sound more like yourself, especially if you are a better verbal story-teller than a writer, is to "tell" your life story before writing it down. This is a method used by many successful professionals who do not write for a living. There are many business leaders who have a hard time writing about what it is that they've accomplished; they sell their products all day long in meetings, on the phone, and at the podium, but they have insecurities about their grammar, and their writing voice sounds nothing like their speaking voice. In their book *The Complete Idiot's Guide to Business Plans*, longtime business coaches Gwen Moran and Sue Johnson suggest that if you are encountering writer's block because you're anxious about putting your thoughts together on paper, you may choose to take out a tape recorder or call a voice mail machine and talk through your story before you write it, transcribing the best of what you've said. You can also talk through what you will say in front of a parent or caring friend before you write down this most personal of stories; the words will sound more natural because your audience will already be receptive and supportive to you.

Editing: Creating Your Masterpiece with Grammar and Style

Now that you have written your essay, you must edit it. This process can be as important, if not more important, than actually writing the essay, which is why you should start writing it far in advance. Your first self-edit should take place forty-eight hours or more after you have written your first draft—give those tired eyes and brain a break! When you come back to it, read it aloud so that you can hear how each sentence flows. Rework each one so that it is short, to the point, and powerful as it can be. For your 400 to 500 word essay, see if you can cut 20 words during your first edit.

If you are preparing to enter college, your command of English should already be well developed, but all of the best writers have a good grammar guide on hand. One of the most concise and beloved of these is the classic *The Elements of Style* by William Strunk and E. B. White, the author of *Charlotte's Web*, which will give you a comforting crash course on writing things clearly, effectively and authentically. In general, the dos of writing include the following:

- Being concise—never use a large word where a short, to-the-point one will do.

- Being concrete—never use a vague word like "good" when you can be more specific: "delicious," "beautiful," "proud," "stunning," "breathtaking" can all mean good, but they say much more.

- Using active voice—this is especially important in an essay where you will show that you did things rather than allowing them to happen to you. Instead of writing, *"I was awarded first prize,"* which sounds humble but almost accidental, write, *"After a hard race, I took first prize."*

- Showing, not telling—instead of saying you are a "good communicator" or a "strong leader," use one sentence to describe a time when you exemplified those qualities: a time you wrote a funny speech to give to your class, or a time when you organized a clothing donation drive for the homeless.

However, if you write either very carelessly, not paying attention to your sentence construction, or write too carefully, cutting and pasting your essay endlessly, you may still end up with a piece of work that is choppy and difficult to read. Overall, you should try not to do the following:

- Switch tenses—a sign of constant editing (*"I walk down the aisle, then turned to face the crowd"*).

- End a sentence with a preposition (*"It was a job I knew I'd be perfect for,"* rather than, *"It was a job for which I knew I'd be perfect"* or *"It was a job I knew I'd love"*).

- Substitute one common part of speech for another (writing "it's" instead of "its," "they're" instead of "their," and "you're" instead of "your").

- Write in run-on sentences rather than breaking them up for easier reading.

After consulting grammar guides and reading your essay through, you are ready to have another person read your essay. While this is not obligatory, we recommend that you do so—having another set of eyes on your essay can reveal errors you haven't noticed because you have seen it so many times.

Consider asking someone who will respect the way you tell your story— you shouldn't have to change it drastically, or your unique voice will be lost. This is why I personally do not recommend online editing services: The editors, while they purport to be "Harvard-educated" and are generally articulate, do not know you personally and often rework things more dramatically than is necessary. Counselors don't want a suspiciously perfect essay with adjectives that just aren't natural to an eighteen-year-old. Harvard degree or no Harvard degree, stick with "editors" who you know and trust.

While your parents might be willing to perform this task, the subject matter may be too close to them—considering it's their child—and they may find themselves unwittingly reacting to the personal nature of the essay, especially if it concerns hard times for your family or your relationships with them. If these things are important to the integrity of your essay, it may be considerate for you to simply tell your parents that you'd prefer that someone without a vested interest in your story read it over.

An English teacher or other trusted advisor is a better choice, because their job involves reading hundreds of essays written by eighteen-year-olds every year, and he or she may already be familiar with your work. Make sure to be open to constructive criticism: Editing is painful for all writers, but it invariably leads to a better piece of writing.

You may also choose to get together and "workshop" your essay with friends, as many professional writers do with their work: Get together on a weekend night, finish your homework in advance so you can concentrate, and pass around copies of everyone's essays so that you can all give each other feedback and encouragement. Knowing that you are not alone in this process will help you overcome your anxiety about this all-important essay.

Above all, know when enough is enough: an overly edited essay is more likely to contain errors through constant cutting and pasting than one that flows organically. Three to four edits should be sufficient: A good writer knows that it's never going to be "perfect." But if it sounds like you, it's already good enough.

To end this chapter, look over the following essays that "made it." Remember, the students that penned these works are like you . . . determined and hopeful.

Below are two sample essays from the same student, Amanda Bergeron. Her college prompted her to write two separate essays—one that would gain her entrance to her first-choice college, Emerson College, and one that would gain her a place in its selective Honors program, as well as a scholarship for $13,000 per year. Even though this was a lot of pressure, especially for someone

College Trivia Quiz #7

This school's football stadium is considered to be the most renowned sports arena in the country. It houses over 80,000 fans. Which school is it?

a) University of Michigan
b) University of Notre Dame
c) Georgia Tech University
d) Harvard University

who had more than one application to complete, she succeeded on both counts. Today, she is the news editor of the newspaper of Emerson College.

We have chosen to show her essays, not only because she has proven herself to be a great writer, but also because seeing them side by side shows that a student may have many different passions to choose from when writing his or her essay—and therefore many viable topics. Amanda's essays show two very different sides of her: One side is an introvert who loves curling up with a book, while the other is an extrovert who plunged herself into passionate community activism. After reading her essays, you may also want to think about which side or sides you will want to show to your college of choice.

Essay 1:

Growing up in Lewiston, Maine, a city whose population is largely Franco-American, I was rarely exposed to any real degree of diversity. My parents always emphasized the importance of respecting and admiring other cultures, ideas, and beliefs. Although I took in these values, I remained sheltered in my Catholic elementary school. It was not until eighth grade that I had the opportunity to form a friendship with someone of a different ethnicity.

Barbara McManus and her young daughter moved to Lewiston from the Bronx because of her husband's job change. A West-Indian woman in a biracial marriage, she was an unusual Lewiston resident at that time. She and my mother became friends, and I would sit near them and listen, enthralled, each time she came over. Born in the West Indies and raised in England, she had seen places that I could only dream of. I was fascinated by the life she had lived and admired the intelligence and confidence she exuded. Sensing my desire to travel and experience new places, Mrs. McManus invited me, much to my delight, to go for an extended weekend trip to New York City with her and her daughter.

When we arrived in the Bronx at her friend's apartment, I was more than a little anxious about the city's reputation, and had no idea what to expect. What I experienced in the next few days was an amazing role reversal. In this predominantly ethnic section of New York City, I was the minority. This idea thrilled me. The array of colors and cultures that I found myself amongst was in stark contrast with my hometown.

Ironically, it was directly after this remarkable cultural experience that I first witnessed the sickening reality of prejudice. On our return trip to Maine, Mrs. McManus was pulled over by a state trooper for speeding, which was odd because the main stream of traffic was flying past us. This officer began to verbally abuse this woman that I so admired. After accepting the unwarranted ticket, and calmly asking for his badge number, she continued driving. Less than thirty seconds after we resumed, he pulled us over a second time. He continued to belittle and threaten her for no apparent reason, with her young daughter crying in the background. I sat there stunned. What I felt after was an inexplicable anger: anger at that man for treating my wonderful friend this way; anger at myself for being helpless to stop it; and anger at a world that would allow such hatred.

This experience compelled me to join the Civil Rights Team at my high school. In the few years that followed, the residents of Lewiston would be challenged in the face of intolerance. Another chance to protect new friends would soon arise.

Beginning my sophomore year, a large group of Somali immigrants arrived in Lewiston. With this new diversity came a threatening adversity. However, our town was ready. Our Civil Rights Team at school tripled in population between my freshman and junior year. Despite a rocky start, friendships were formed between native and new residents. When a hate group called the World Church of the Creator tried to threaten the safety of our new friends, our community was prepared. We stood together in unity against prejudice and further strengthened our relationships.

Lewiston, Maine, is becoming less of the homogenous community it once was, and the residents are beginning to be more accepting of a wider spectrum of colors, religions, and traditions. The two events that I have experienced of diversity in the face of intolerance have allowed me to realize something crucial: the world is not always just and it does contain hatred, yet it is each person's responsibility to protect the beauty of diversity from those who threaten it.

Essay 2:

Curled up next to my mother on the old brown couch, with a lamp softly illuminating the pages of a book, I discovered a world with which I would instantly fall in love. My mother believed she was sharing her love of literature with me, but she was truly giving me much more. This early introduction into the world of books awoke in me my love for the written word.

Throughout my early childhood, I grasped at every opportunity to read, my mind greedy for every adventure, every mystery, and every character. While most parents needed to monitor their children's time in front of the television, mine needed to limit my time reading books. I remember many nights when I would wait anxiously in my bed for my parents to think I was asleep so I could turn on my lamp and resume my reading.

It was magic to me that words on a page could convey such energy and depth. I was in awe of authors and their ability to evoke such strong emotions in me. In second grade I realized, with the help of my teacher, Mrs. Graham, that perhaps I might also learn to acquire this power. One day, my teacher assigned us the task of writing a Halloween story, which I excitedly completed. The praise that followed from my beloved teacher lit a fire within me that spurred me to continue writing. It was this second grade experience that fueled my desire to take my love of the written word and express myself with it.

Although I continued writing, I spent much of the next eight or nine years adding to the library in my head, reading anything that came my way. During this period, I also fell in and out of love with countless other forms of self-expression—none lasting very long and each dying quickly like a short-lived flame. First, I was enticed by ballet and the complexity of emotions that can be conveyed by allowing oneself to be consumed by the music. Next, I tried playing the piano. After that, I was consumed by love of the stage and the thrill of becoming any character at any moment. These passions each lasted for a few years and still hold special places in my heart, yet none could ever fulfill me the way writing does.

It was by chance or perhaps by fate, that in an elective course, sophomore year, my first love once again took center stage. The rush I had felt from a blank page—waiting, begging to be filled—came back to me in an instant. I felt guilty, as if I had slighted my love for nearly a decade, until I realized that my other, temporary passions had enriched my mind, creating a new palette of ideas for me. In retrospect, I was never unfaithful to my passion of writing; Instead, I had been waiting for a time when I could handle its complexity.

After spending a period drifting from one experience to another, I found that my first love has always been my only. Now, looking into the future, I believe that I need an education that will allow me to further develop my skills, to explore my passion, and to obtain all the tools necessary to follow my ambition of becoming a journalist, and to achieve my goal of becoming an established author. My education started on the old brown couch, and I would love for it to be continued at Emerson College.

College Clues and Cues

Colleges would not ask you to write an essay if they were not interested in the creative, expressive part of your mind. So use it! Don't be afraid to go beyond the formulas we give you to show them your talent—even beyond the typical written essay. If you are a poet, go ahead and use this medium to express yourself with a personal verse or two—as long the composition on the whole still answers the question, gives counselors a sense of who you really are, includes details about your background and accomplishments, and includes their school in some way. If you are applying to an art school, you may already be asked to provide samples of your work, but these might also be appropriate to send to mainstream schools as well if they accomplish the same task as the essay: showing something that defines you in a way that your test scores do not.

During the days when applications were sent in by mail, it wasn't uncommon for students to enclose artwork or photos; today, most applications are online, but if you have another art form that you use to express yourself, you may consider giving the admissions department a call to see if you may mail supporting materials along with your application to be included in your folder. For example, if your passion is stand-up comedy, ask if they'd like to see a DVD of your performance to accompany your essay on it. What about that collage you spent months on? Ask if you can fax them a photo. At the very worst, the staffer will say, "No, thank you, your application is strong enough already." And at the best, you will impress them with your eagerness—and even more when they see your work. Consider it practice for college and the "real world," where you can't afford to be shy when it comes to promoting your best product and your most important client—yourself.

College Clues and Cues
For Parents

Take a trip online and you will find a wealth of people that can promise your son or daughter admission to an Ivy League school by boosting their credentials, raising their SAT scores, and writing their essays for them. All you need to do is send them part of your own wealth. Do you need this? Probably not.

The majority of colleges and universities interviewed for this book said that they were looking for the voices of eighteen-year-olds . . . young adults that needed their kind of schooling. One admissions staff member even said, "We want the essay to have a mistake or two . . . it's after they graduate that there should not be mistakes."

There may be a temptation to send your future scholar to test reviews, coaching sessions for interviews, and writing labs for essays. If your son or daughter had difficulties in writing during high school or gets test anxiety, perhaps these extra courses will be helpful. But in general, if your son or daughter is college material, having at least a 2.5 GPA, has tended to follow through on their projects, and seems enthusiastic about interviewing for the college of their choice, talk with them and see what they need from you. This book has provided you with enough information and preparatory material to become your own facilitator of college information gathering and deadlines. To keep the light in your offspring's eyes, don't assume that to compete he or she needs coaching outside of school. Instead, let him or her tell you what is needed.

8

How to Impress, Express, and Dress at College Interviews

Eighty percent of success is showing up.
—Woody Allen

Remember Alice's dilemma at the opening of chapter 2? She wasn't sure where she was going and the Cheshire Cat was of little help to her. (She had also been shrunk down to microscopic size.) What Alice should have said when asked where she was going and why was:

> *I plan on attending the University of Wisconsin at Milwaukee for their excellent chemistry program. Perhaps then, I can configure something to help me get back to my normal size. Can you give me information on how many chemistry majors attend the University of Wisconsin and what jobs the graduates have obtained?*

Her answer would probably have impressed the admissions staff member that interviewed Alice because her answer was confident and knowledgeable, and *she* asked a question of the admissions staff member. Rather impressive.

The Guidance Services website of Peters Township High School in Mc-Murray, Pennsylvania, provides their students with the following excellent suggestions for preparing for college interviews:

Research the college by visiting the college's web site and/or reading the college catalog. Make sure to review sections dealing with your intended major and/or programs in which you hope to become involved. Your expression of interest in the college will not come from merely stating those words, but in actuality, your knowledge of the school and its programs that you have researched.

Besides the mental preparation, there is another kind of preparation that you must attend to. How you present yourself and answer questions in a confident manner will resonate with the admissions staff. To help you through, check out the following tips for dressing, expressing, and impressing everyone.

Dress for Success

No matter what major you are going to work toward, your attire should be "business casual," unless it is stated otherwise. If you are really concerned, call the admissions office and inquire: "What is the dress code for college interviews?" This way you will know for sure. Typically, though, for guys, business casual means a nice pair of slacks (no jeans) and either a polo shirt tucked in with a belt or a button down shirt, tie optional. If you are applying to an Ivy League school, you might add the tie. Wear dress shoes or loafers with socks. No sandals. If you have a spare binder that you can carry, slip in your résumé (more about that later) and some loose-leaf paper so that you can take notes. Clip a pen inside so you don't have to search for one. Take the school catalogue with you. This way you will look prepared.

For girls, wear a conservative blouse, with a skirt or slacks (no jeans). Forget low-cut or spaghetti-strapped blouses. Sweaters are great if the season allows. Choose shoes that you would wear to a church-type event, closed toe being preferable to open toed sandals. Carry a purse and the same binder as the guys with a résumé, catalogue, paper, and pen. If you are going to play a musical instrument as part of your interview, make sure your clothing is comfortable enough to move in.

What to Take

If you are an athlete and you are being interviewed by a college coaching team, take your scrapbook with newspaper clippings, programs, statistics, or any other information that will describe you on paper.

If you are interested in majoring in art, photography, film, or any other media, including journalism, take a portfolio. Ask your teacher to advise you on how to arrange your work in a portfolio. Go an art store to get an oversized "binder" that your work can fit into. If you are interested in photography, ask your teacher or the art teacher to help you mat your photos. If you are interested in film, ask your media tech teacher to help you make a "reel," which can be a DVD that you compose, edit, and fill with your work.

If You Have a Disability

If you have a physical *disability*, make sure that when you set the date for the interview the facility will accommodate your needs. On the day of the interview, stay confident that the school has other students with differences and that the interviewer will expect to do what he/she needs to do to make you comfortable.

If you mentioned on your application that you have a learning disability, at the end of the interview, ask about study labs for students with your particular disability. Most colleges are required by law to accommodate students with learning disabilities so that they can be successful. By finding out this information, you will be more comfortable with your admission and knowing the procedures will make your first few weeks easier.

Impress Them: Flattery Will Get You Everywhere!

Think about it. In the same way that you are flattered when a peer notices something that you did well, colleges notice when you can cite their successful programs. As you prepare for your college interview, look up your intended major and learn about the variety of classes that you can take. In most college catalogues you will find a full description of the class. Using your highlighter, highlight the classes that intrigue you. Take the catalogue with you and when it's your turn to ask a question, refer to a highlighted section. Again, planning and organization impresses people.

When you want to impress someone, you plan ahead of time how you will do that. The following ideas are a compilation of information that I received when researching college interview strategies:

1. Arrive early to campus, even the day before if the college is out of town. You can look at the campus, visit with other students, and get familiar with the territory. Even if you do not live far, arrive early. Most of the interviews are scheduled back to back so if you arrive a few minutes late, not only will you make a poor impression to begin with, you will have less time with the interviewer. Besides, there might be paperwork to complete.

2. Greet the interviewer by shaking his or her hand. Smile and show your appreciation for the invitation to interview. Thank the interviewer for seeing you and try to get to know him or her by looking carefully around the office for pictures and graduation diplomas on the wall. By gaining some rapport, you will come to see the interviewer as another adult that likes students. This is calming. Also, maintain a good eye contact during the interview. This is a sign of respect and many people also believe it is a sign of maturity and sincerity. If your interview is with more than one person, address each of them as you speak, looking from person to person.

3. After you are invited into the office, wait until the interviewer sits before you sit. This is a politeness that makes you look quite professional.

4. Bring a binder and some pens to the interview. Inside the binder, have paper and a copy of your résumé that you developed in the last chapter. The interviewer might ask for the résumé and you will be prepared. Keep a copy of the college catalogue with you, too, in case you want to refer to it when you are asking your own questions.

5. Speak clearly. When you are asked questions and have a difficult time understanding them, don't hesitate to ask for clarification. Take the time to answer the question, and answer it in words that sound confident and relaxed. Be yourself. If you need the interviewer to rephrase the question or repeat it, try the following response: *"Would you mind repeating the question? I am not quite sure what you are asking."*

6. Display honesty along with confidence as you answer questions. If you wonder about taking four courses of French, mention that it is a little challenging but that you are up to it. Take a positive approach that shows a lot of hope and determination, even if the course load is challenging. You want your chance!

7. If you think the interview went well, ask the interviewer when you might get an answer regarding admission. This again shows your enthusiasm and your appreciation for the interview and for being considered as a student.

8. Take a business card from the interviewer and once you arrive home, write a personal thank-you note. Don't e-mail it and don't print it on your computer. Write it in your own handwriting.

Express Yourself: The Interview Questions

Your interview will be your chance to put your face to a stack of application papers and recommendation letters. In addition to being your charming self, you should prepare yourself to have a conversation with someone that simply wants to know why you belong on his short stack of admissions rather than his tall stack of "waiting list" applicants. Prepare for the interview by practicing. On the next few pages you will find a group of questions commonly asked by an admissions staff member that we will refer to as the "interviewer."

Practice can also alleviate quite a bit of anxiety, particularly when you surround yourself with comforting, encouraging people. To begin practicing, think about how you have practiced for other situations in your high school career, whether it was sports, music, or any other kind of competition. In addition to going through the motions until you "got it," you probably did some things to pump yourself up. Use those strategies here as well.

Choose an audience to practice your interview performance for that you trust to give you clear and kind feedback about your answers. Your parents are a good choice because they can help with answers on personal questions since they know you best. Tell them that you want their comments, not their coaching or suggestions. This needs to be your wordage. Your teachers can help you on the academic questions. The rest is up to you. By researching the college catalogue, which was mentioned earlier, and practicing some answers, you will appear more calm and confident and that will impress them.

Annie's Interview

Annie is a high school senior with aspirations to be a high school English teacher. She became quite anxious when she received a letter inviting her to interview for an elite, private college tucked away in Massachusetts. To curb her nerves, but not her enthusiasm, she visited with her English teacher, her newspaper sponsor, and her parents. And she practiced what to say so that there would be a few less surprises for her.

The following is a list of questions that I have compiled from a variety of

College Trivia Quiz #8

Which school's marching band formed the first letter on a football field in 1907?

a) University of Illinois
b) Purdue University
c) Washington State University
d) University of California, Los Angeles

admissions staff members. They are considered typical questions asked of college interviewers. By reviewing them, you will be very well prepared for whatever the interviewer asks. These are just *examples* of how Annie (or you!) might answer them. You have your own unique ways of answering them.

1. Why do you want to go to college?

"I would like to have a career as an English teacher and to do that, I need a college degree. I was also influenced by my AP English teacher last year, who encouraged me to begin writing essays. Hopefully as an English major, I will learn more about writing and possibly try my hand at submitting articles for publication someday."

2. Why have you selected our college?

"I began researching colleges for their English majors in my junior year of high school and liked the quotes that your students provided on the website about the English department. I have also met an alumnus of your university who enjoyed her time here. The courses that are outlined in the catalogue seem to fit what I am interested in. I also like the size of the university and the location."

3. What are your career plans? If you are uncertain about your plans, don't be afraid to say so. If you are, what is it about this college that you like?

"Right now, I am aiming to be a high school English teacher. I am also very interested in writing for publication as I learn new writing skills in college."

4. What was the latest book that you read?

"The latest book that I read was Girlfriends. *I have lots of friends that I have enjoyed in high school and it was interesting for me to read about how the author saw girlfriends and their intertwined, crazy relationships. I actually gave the book to a few of my friends to read and they loved it, too."*

5. Do you have any special hobbies or talents?

"I ran track each spring, mostly cross-country, while I was in middle school and in high school. I was never really into contact sports but I have always loved to run. During my junior and senior year we went to the state competition and in my senior year my school placed second. I also love to read historical accounts of famous women. I am fascinated by successful females and how they contributed to our country's history."

6. What do you like most about this college?

"I had the chance to walk around the campus before our interview and visit the buildings that I read about in your brochure online. I was very impressed by how friendly the students were to me. I even had a chance to talk to some of them about how they liked attending school here. The school spirit was all very positive. I think that the campus makes me feel at home and to me, that will make me comfortable to really study.

"In addition, I love the courses that are outlined in the school catalogue for English majors. I have researched the reputation of the faculty and noticed that they also take students abroad to study in Europe each summer. That sounds really fascinating to me."

7. Tell me a little about yourself.

"I am the third child in my family, and the only daughter. I have two older twin brothers, so being the younger sister has been interesting! I always had protection! My parents both graduated from colleges and my older brothers finished college last year. I am the last one to leave home! I have always enjoyed reading and writing, and during high school was able to write for the school newspaper. I attend the Methodist church in my hometown where I volunteer in the nursery on Sundays. I like music, hanging out with my girlfriends, my boyfriend, and my family."

8. What do you have to offer our college?

"My English teacher said that my essays were unusually funny and insightful. She said I had a different kind of 'voice' to my writing. I would like to contribute to the school newspaper and maybe meet with and work with Dr. Kendall, an English professor in your English department that specializes in humorous essays. I read some of his essays online on his faculty webpage and couldn't stop laughing.

"I think I will also offer friendship to my dorm roommates. I will contribute to class discussions. I would like to make the university proud by entering into writing competitions and representing this school."

9. Who do you admire the most, and why?

"I admire several people. I admire my parents for working hard to be successful. My mother is a psychologist and my father is an engineer. They both worked very hard when I was growing up and always explained what they did in their jobs to me and to my brothers. I think it motivated us to be like them.

"I admire my grandfather. He is eighty-three and still mows his yard and walks three miles a day. He never gives up on anything he starts. He always taught me to do the same.

"Finally, I admire my English teacher. I had never had a teacher like him. He not only encouraged us to complete our assignments, he would help us to submit our work for competitions. When we won, he would celebrate with us and make sure the news was announced all over the school. When we lost, he would sit with us and explain that the life of a writer is sometimes filled with disappointment but that disappointment can turn into a new essay."

10. What are your strongest points?

"My strongest points are that I have my parents' and my grandfather's perseverance and strong will! I also love to read and I can be a really good friend to someone. When I believe in a good cause I will work hard to help out someone who needs help. Usually when I decide to do something, I follow through, even if things get difficult and challenging."

11. What would you like to change about yourself?

"I would like to have more confidence. As the youngest in my family, I have been taken care of but at times, I think I was taken care of too much. Now that I get to go to college, I have a chance to prove myself. That's what I want to change while I am here."

These answers are fictional, but Annie was just as candid, personable, honest, and extremely enthusiastic with her actual answers. In college interviews, the interviewer will listen for passion and determination like Annie explained she had. The interviewer will also be impressed that Annie researched Dr. Kendall, the English professor that writes humorous essays. This kind of excitement should come across to the interviewer. When it does, you will impress them.

Questions *You* Should Ask *Them*

Another fact that I learned about when interviewing college admissions staff members was their interest in being asked questions by students. Remember, they are similar to a matchmaker, so to make sure you "fit" with them and they "fit" with you, they want as much conversation as possible. Asking questions also makes you appear very interested in their university, and that's flattering. Look at the list of questions below. Practice asking these questions to your family and teachers. See if the questions fit with what you are curious about. If not, add your own, omit some, keeping the flavor of academic curiosity . . . also known as your desire to succeed in their university.

1. When will I begin taking classes in my major?

2. Will my advisor be a faculty member in my major's department?

3. When will I visit with my advisor?

4. Does _____ college have internships that students can participate in? What semester do students usually do their internships?

5. Does _____ college help students get jobs after graduation? How does that work?

6. Do students at _____ college typically join sororities and fraternities? What type of national clubs are here on campus?

7. Do most students live on campus?

8. Does _____ college offer study abroad programs?

9. What do you consider as most important in the admission process?

10. Are most first-year courses taught by professors or by teaching assistants?

11. How are the computer equipment and library resources? When is the library open?

12. I am interested in scholarships if I am admitted. Can you direct me to a form that I need to complete?

In the appendix, you will find an Interview Cheat Sheet that you can take with you in your binder. By asking these questions you will come across as a student that has already done your college homework.

College Clues and Cues

Think of your college interview as a conversation with an adult that is interested in learning who you are. It's not a test, it's not a survey to listen to how many "ums" you say or a chance to trick you into saying something that will disqualify you. It's a time to see if you fit the college and the college fits you.

Chances are that you have interviewed for a job, a position with the student council, or with your school counselor in the past. How did you manage those situations? In fact, as you drive to the interview ask yourself about the good risks that you have taken for the past eighteen years of your life and how they turned out positively. Ask yourself what you believed about yourself that pushed you to perform. Ask yourself how you felt afterward. These same abilities will work this time . . . it's just another conversation.

College Clues and Cues
For Parents

She's rather grown up, in her business-casual outfit, binder and college catalogue in hand. You don't have to braid her hair or tie her shoes anymore. In fact, during the next year, you won't have to wash her clothes or tell her to put the rubber bands on her braces. She's ready to interview at the college she dreams of attending. Your job? Sit there, listen, and believe.

It's really tempting to coach our kids on what to say when spoken to. We've had experiences where, to get the right job, we had to say the right things. Luckily, this interview is not going to make or break the admission, really. Most college interviewers that I spoke with said that when they do interviews, they already have an idea if admission is a possibility or not. Perhaps it is the college's procedure to interview. Perhaps there is a wait list and to decide who gets in this year, an interview will do the trick. But it is a combination of your future scholar's performance in the classroom, at the testing site, on the field, in the community, and at home with her sister that will help the admission interviewer decide.

So when you see her climb the stairs, stay in the car. Don't follow her. Take a book to read and tell her you will be waiting. Tell her you love her and that you know she's going to do great. And she probably will.

CONCLUSION

I have a cousin that graduated from Texas A&M years ago with a major in public relations. The first year after she graduated, she landed a high-paying job in Dallas and within a year was promoted. Her secret? Whenever she approached a new company, she would find out who worked in the company that graduated from A&M and requested to meet with that person first. With the help of that person, she began her relationship with the firm. She always walked away the winner.

As a high school student, you might wonder what buddying up with an alumnus might have to do with a promotion. Let's just say that the loyalty of university alums is one of the strongest ties you will ever experience. Why else would people don ridiculous hats and paint their faces green and purple and gold and keep their fraternity jersey in their cedar chest all of their lives? It's because the college experience is the experience of a lifetime. A time when you will grow from an adolescent that can't declare a major to a young adult that recognizes a future full of possibilities. And you don't do all of this alone. You do it with people that may become your best friends, spouse, and colleagues for life.

By now, you have read about the application process, the tests to take, the résumés to write, the financial aid forms to complete, and the interview questions that will win you admission. But what you haven't read about are the experiences that only you can and will have during the coming years. Count them among the most important experiences you will have in your life. Count them among experiences where you will learn more about yourself than you ever thought possible. This is a time when life opens its doors and welcomes you into a new world. Future college graduate, welcome to the best years of your life! Enjoy.

APPENDIX

REFERENCES

ACT Publications

www.act.org

The Associated Press, October 12, 2004

Carroll, Lewis (2000). *Alice's Adventures in Wonderland and Through the Looking-Glass.* Signet Publishers.

Central Wyoming College, 2006

www.collegeboard.com

www.commonapp.org

de Shazer, S. (1985). *Keys to Solution in Brief Therapy.* W. W. Norton & Company.

Columbia University undergraduate application, 2006–2007

The Daily Targum, Rutgers University, 2000

www.fafsa.org

Gill, J. (2006). Continental.com magazine, pp. 71–75.

www.intensivewriting.com

www.ivybound.net

Journal of American College Health, 2002

Lord, L. (1997). "From Party Hearty to Party Hardly?" *U.S. News & World Report*, p. 24.

Massachusetts Institute of Technology undergraduate application, 2006–2007

McGrath, A. (2006). *America's Best Colleges, U.S. News & World Report 2006 Edition*, p. 10.

Metcalf, L. (2005). *The Miracle Question.* Crown House Publishers.

Moran, G., and Johnson, S. (2005). *The Complete Idiot's Guide to Business Plans*. Penguin Books.

"100 Best Colleges" (2006). *U.S. News & World Report*.

Peters Township High School (www.ptsd.k12.pa.us)

www.princetonreview.com

www.sparknotes.com

www.usnews.com

Wheatt, D. (2006). "SAT/ACT Scores and College Admissions. How Much Is Your Score Really Worth?" www.collegeview.com.

COLLEGE TRIVIA QUIZ ANSWERS

1. B. Vassar College is the alma mater of both Téa Leoni and Lisa Kudrow. Oberlin College was never a women's college, though it has the distinction of being the first coeducational college in the United States Hunter College was founded as a teacher-training school for women, but became fully coeducational in 1964. Radcliffe became part of Harvard University, while Vassar began admitting men in 1969. Goucher College began as the Women's College of Baltimore, but was renamed Goucher College in 1910. (www.princetonreview.com)

2. A. Memphis. The University of Memphis is one of Tennessee's three comprehensive doctoral-extensive institutions of higher learning. Situated in a beautiful parklike setting in the state's largest city, it is the flagship of the Tennessee Board of Regents system. It awards more than 3,000 degrees annually. With an enrollment of approximately 21,000 students, The University of Memphis has twenty-five Chairs of Excellence, more than any other Tennessee university, and five state-approved Centers of Excellence. (www.memphis.edu)

3. Each president and John Lithgow graduated from Harvard University. John Adams graduated from Harvard College in 1755 and, for a time, taught school in Worcester and studied law. He also had a tutor. John Quincy Adams entered Harvard College and graduated in 1787. He was then admitted to the bar association and began practicing law in Boston, Massachusetts. John Kennedy began attending Harvard College in 1936. After graduating Harvard, he attended Stanford University's business school for a few months. John Lithgow graduated magna cum laude from Harvard College in 1967, then received a Fulbright Scholarship after graduation to study at the London Academy of Music and Dramatic Art.

4. B. Harvard University.

5. Known as Lew Alcindor in 1965 when he was leading Power Memorial Academy of New York City to seventy-two straight high school wins. Later as an NBA star he would change his name to Kareem Abdul-Jabbar.

6. Madonna. Two years into her college studies, Madonna grew impatient for the stage and fame and dropped out of college. She moved to New York where there is a legend that she sat down in Times Square with only $35 in her pocket. Working behind the counter at the Times Square Dunkin' Donuts, the dancer turned to singing and began writing songs and learned to play the piano and the guitar.

7. In 1997, Notre Dame Stadium had a major renovation and addition that raised the capacity for its fans to 80,000. It is actually considered to be the most up-to-date football facility in the nation today.

8. Purdue University's marching band first formed a letter on a football field in 1907.

COLLEGE FACT SHEET

BASIC FACTS

Name of College: _____

Phone: _____

Address for Admissions: _____

_____

_____

Admissions Phone: _____

Admissions E-mail: _____

Financial Aid Phone: _____

Financial Aid E-mail: _____

Housing Phone: _____

Housing E-mail: _____

Registrar Phone: _____

Registrar E-mail: _____

ITEM	DATE OF ACTION	ITEM INFORMATION SENT TO SCHOOL (YES/NO)	DATE RESPONSE NEEDED	ITEMS COMPLETED
Application				
Application fee				
SAT test				
ACT test				
Housing application				
Housing deposit				
FAFSA				
Admission deposit				
Transcript				
Recommendation letters requested				
Recommendation letters sent				

RECOMMENDATION LETTER REQUEST

Dear Teacher,

I am applying to college for the _____ school year. I plan on majoring in
_____. Your recommendation is very important to me. Please write a letter
of recommendation for me to the following school(s):

_____

_____

_____

_____

_____

For your assistance, I am enclosing the following documents:

1. Experience Worksheet

2. Résumé

3. A Format for Recommendation Letters

4. Envelopes (one is addressed to the college, the other to me, for my records)

Thank you for writing this letter for me. Your help is appreciated. Please send the letter by
_____, the deadline that the college has set for my application.

Sincerely,

Name: _____

Student ID#: _____

Student e-mail: _____

A FORMAT FOR RECOMMENDATION LETTERS

Paragraph #1: Recommend the student for admission to the university. Write about the number of years that you have known the student and in what capacity.

Paragraph #2: Discuss the student's activities academically and any other activities that contribute to the student's character. Mention unique qualities about this student that separates the student from other applicants. Write about personal experiences that you had with the student in regard to academic diligence and success. Mention how these assets will serve the student well throughout his/her college career. Add comments on your confidence that this student will succeed in the major that he/she has chosen to study.

Paragraph #3: Give your professional opinion about this student and recommend her for admission to the university. Mention how the student will add to the campus community and how he/she will be a prosperous student that will graduate and represent the school well in the future.

INTERVIEW CHEAT SHEET

1. When will I begin taking classes in my major?
2. Will my advisor be a faculty member in my major's department?
3. When will I visit with my advisor?
4. Does _____ college have internships that students can participate in? What semester do students usually do their internships?
5. Does _____ college help students get jobs after graduation? How does that work?
6. Do students at _____ college typically join sororities and fraternities? What type of national clubs are here on campus?
7. Do most students live on campus?
8. Does _____ college offer study abroad programs?
9. What do you consider as most important in the admission process?
10. Are most first-year courses taught by professors or by teaching assistants?
11. How are the computer equipment and library resources? When is the library open?
12. I am interested in scholarships if I am admitted. Can you direct me to a form that I need to complete?

REQUEST FOR HIGH SCHOOL TRANSCRIPT

Dear Registrar,

I am applying to college for the _____ school year. Please send a copy of my transcript to the following school:

_____

_____

_____

_____

_____

My information:

Name: _____

Student ID #: _____

Social Security #: _____

Date of Birth: _____

Address: _____

City: _____   State: _____   Zip: _____

Thank you very much.

GLOSSARY

ACT—A test that assesses high school students' general educational development and their ability to complete college-level work. The multiple-choice tests cover four skill areas: English, mathematics, reading, and science. The optional Writing Test is a thirty-minute essay test that measures students' writing skills in English.

Adjunct professor—An instructor with at least a master's degree and preferably a doctoral degree that is hired to teach an individual course, during a specific semester.

AP—Advanced Placement courses that are offered to high school students, enabling them to get college credit while still attending high school, upon successful completion of the AP exam. These classes involve a more rigorous academic curriculum than regular education classes.

Assistant professor—The entry-level position, for which one usually needs a PhD or other doctorate; a master's degree may suffice, especially at community colleges or in fields for which there is a terminal master's degree.

Associate's degree—a two-year degree, often offered at a community college, that prepares a student for a career and includes academic course requirements, such as math, English, and science along with courses in the career field. Once an associate's degree is complete, a person may decide to go to work in the chosen field or transfer to a four-year university to complete a bachelor's degree.

Associate professor—The mid-level position, usually awarded after obtaining tenure. In relatively rare circumstances, a person may be hired at the associate professor level without tenure. Typically this is done as a financial inducement to attract someone from outside the institution.

Bachelor's degree—An undergraduate academic degree awarded for a course or major that generally lasts for three, four, or in some cases and countries, five or six years.

CEEB/ACT code—The college entrance exam code that is required to register to take the ACT or SAT test. This code is typically available from the school counselor.

Class rank—A student's position in a graduating class determined by the student's cumulative grade point averages (GPA).

College—An institution of higher learning, not always a university, that grants the undergraduate bachelor's degree in liberal arts or science or both.

College advisor—A staff member of a university whose position is dedicated to helping students design a degree plan for graduation. Students are often assigned to their own individual college advisor. In many colleges, a student switches to an advisor in his/her major toward the end of their college career.

Common Application—A standardized undergraduate college application form that is accepted at more than 240 accredited, independent colleges and universities nationwide.

CSS/PROFILE—The financial aid application service of the College Board. More than 600 colleges, universities, graduate and professional schools, and scholarship programs use the information collected on the PROFILE to determine eligibility for nonfederal student aid funds.

Degree plan—A plan for graduation, usually constructed with an academic advisor, that includes required courses in addition to courses required in a particular major.

Disability—Refers to psychological and neurological conditions that affect a person's communicative capacities and potential to be taught effectively. The term includes such conditions as dysgraphia (writing disorder), dyslexia (reading disorder), dyscalculia (mathematics disorder) and developmental aphasia.

Doctoral Degree—Typically a doctor of philosophy, or PhD, is awarded to a person completing more than 100 hours of graduate school and a formal dissertation. The dissertation is a written manuscript describing a formal research study.

EA—Early action programs for college admissions that allow students to apply ahead of time, but do not require that students attend the university

ED—Early decision for admission to a university implies that if a student is admitted to the school, they will attend and withdraw their other college applications.

Extracurricular activities—Activities performed by students that fall outside the realm of the normal curriculum of school or university education.

FAFSA—The Free Application for Federal Student Aid is document enabling students to apply online for student financial aid that includes student loans and scholarships. Once completed, universities selected by the student to receive the data process the request for student aid.

FERPA—The Family Educational Rights and Privacy Act is a Federal law that protects the privacy of student education records. The law applies to all schools that receive funds under an applicable program of the U.S. Department of Education. FERPA gives parents certain rights with respect to their children's education records. These rights transfer to the student when he or she reaches the age of 18 or attends a school beyond the high school level.

Full professor—A professor who holds tenure and is virtually immune to dismissal and has an appointment for life. The reason for the existence of tenure is the principle of academic freedom, which holds that it is beneficial for state, society, and academe in the long run if professors are free to hold and advance controversial views without fear of losing their jobs.

GED—Stands for "general equivalency diploma" that is awarded to a person who passes an exam on high school subjects. A person with a GED can attend a community college and later, a university, based on the college GPA.

GPA (weighted)—This term refers to courses that were given extra grade points by the school, such as in an honors, AP, or IB class that is more rigorous in curriculum requirements. These extra grade points may be added to the student's final GPA.

Hazing—An often ritualistic test, which may constitute harassment, abuse, or humiliation with requirements to perform meaningless tasks; sometimes as a way of initiation into a social group.

Legacy—Generally defined as having a mother, grandmother, father, or grandfather that was a member of a certain sorority or fraternity. Each club has its own definition of legacy and its application for membership.

Master's degree—a graduate degree that is obtained typically after completion of a bachelor's degree and requires two or more years of study in a specialized area. The master's degree often opens the door to many career opportunities that are personally, professionally, and financially fulfilling.

Panhellenic—A term that means "all Greek," and is a national organization that helps to further aim the purposes of sororities and fraternities.

Pledging—A time when a new member has been selected by a sorority or fraternity and must go through a process for membership.

PSAT NMSQT—The Preliminary SAT/National Merit Scholarship Qualifying Test. It's a standardized test that provides firsthand practice for the SAT Reasoning Test. It also gives you a chance to enter National Merit Scholarship Corporation (NMSC) scholarship programs.

Regular admission—Refers to admission by a college or university based on its receipt of an application, high school transcripts, optional letters of recommendation, and GPA as required by the institution by a specific date.

Rolling admission—Refers to admission by a college or university based on its receipt of an application, high school transcripts, optional letters of recommendation, and GPA as required by the institution, throughout the school year, with no specific date.

Rush—A formal process taken by a sorority or fraternity of a college that is designed to help current members choose new members for their club.

SAT—A standardized test, formally called the Scholastic Aptitude Test and Scholastic Assessment Test, frequently used by colleges and universities in the United States to aid in the selection of incoming freshmen.

SAT I—A three-hour, primarily multiple-choice test that measures verbal and mathematical reasoning abilities that develop over time. Most colleges require SAT I scores for admission.

SAT II—The "subject" tests are one hour, primarily multiple-choice tests that measure your knowledge of particular subjects and your ability to apply that knowledge. Many universities may require this test along with the SAT I.

Scholarship/grant—A specific program that provides financial assistance to a student attending a college or university that is awarded to the student based on his/her assets, need or merit. A scholarship or grant does not require repayment.

Student loan—Refers to financial assistance given by a college or university from federal or nonfederal funding that is intended to be used for educational purposes only. The student loan must be repaid, yet is often deferred until six months after a student graduates or is no longer enrolled in study.

TOEFL—Test of English as a Foreign Language. The TOEFL test opens more doors than any other academic English test. More than 6,000 institutions and agencies in 110 countries rely on TOEFL scores to select students with the English skills needed to succeed.

University—An institution for higher learning with teaching and research facilities constituting a graduate school and professional schools that award master's degrees and doctorates and an undergraduate division that awards bachelor's degrees.

PREPARATORY BOOKS
FOR COLLEGE TESTS

The Official SAT Study Guide
The College Board

This is the only book that features new SAT practice tests created by the test maker. It's packed with the information students need to get ready for the exam. Students will gain valuable experience by taking eight practice tests and receiving estimated scores.

SAT Subject Test: Literature 2006–2007 Edition (Kaplan SAT Subject Tests: Literature)
Kaplan

This book provides a focused review of literary terms, as well as practice questions in each chapter that include working with poetry, fiction, nonfiction, and play excerpts.

Crash Course for the ACT, Third Edition (College Test Prep)
Princeton Review

This book contains strategies that you must know for the exam and dozens of practice questions that you can use to master the techniques given in the book. There are also extensive explanations of the answers so students understand the concepts and don't make the same mistakes twice.

12 Practice Tests for the AP Exams (College Test Prep)
Princeton Review

This compilation of practice tests helps you prepare for multiple Advanced Placement exams. It includes practice exams in the most popular AP subject areas tested, including U.S. History, Biology, English Literature, English Language, Calculus, and U.S. Government, as well as detailed answer explanations.

INDEX

Page numbers in *italics* indicate forms.

PCTA
Library Media Center
41 Fricker Street
Providence, RI 02903